Taqiyyah

Grounds, Concepts, and Limitations

Āyatullāh Jaʿfar Subḥānī

AL-BURĀQ

Copyright

ISBN: 978-1-956276-34-3
Printed and published by al-Burāq Publications.
Translated and annotated by al-Burāq Publications.
Where needed, context and transliterations were added. Some minor edits were made to the translated Arabic text.

Ordering Information
We offer discounts and promotions for wholesale purchases, non-profit organizations, and other educational institutions. Contact us at the email below for further information.

www.al-Buraq.org
publications@al-Buraq.org

First Edition | March 2023

Dedication

The publication of this book was made possible through the generous support of our donors.

Please recite *Sūrat al-Fātiha* and ask God for the Divine reward (*thawāb*) to be conferred upon the donors and also the souls of all the deceased in whose memory their loved ones have contributed graciously towards the publication of *Taqiyyah*.

We begin by giving all praise and thanks to God ﷻ for giving us the *tawfīq* to translate this book. He has guided us and without Him, we would not have been guided to the straight path embodied by the Prophet Muḥammad ﷺ and the Ahl al-Bayt عليهم السلام.

This book is dedicated to all the scholars, martyrs and believers who worked tirelessly to promote the pure Muḥammadan path.

We want to also give our thanks and appreciation to all believers from around the world and acknowledge the team which helped al-Burāq Publications complete this work, spending countless hours to make its publication possible. Please recite *Sūrat al-Fātiḥah* on behalf of them, their families, and their marḥūmīn.

This book is dedicated in honor of the following individuals. Please remember them in your prayers and may God ﷻ have mercy on them and their loved ones.

Abbas

Abda Khalil

Ahmad H. Taleb

Ali Ftouni

Alihussain

Alya Agemy

Bande Khuda

Hajj Ahmad Sheet

Hajj Hassan Sobh

Hajj Nabil Charara

Hajj Sami Ftouni

Hajji Amneh Sobh-Ftouni

Hajji Hiam Hojeije

Hajji Imane Srour

Hajji Samia Srour

Hajji Zahya Fawaz

Humayun Ali Baig

Khadija Fayad

Layla Messelmani

Mariam Al Haj Hussein

Mujtaba Rizvi

Mustafa Hashemi

Qasimhasan

Sayyid Sobh H. Sobh

Shahīd Ibrahim Hadi

Shahīd Sayyid Arif H. al-Husayni

Syed Abul Hassan Bokhari

Syed Mohammed H. Bokhari

Syed Mujtaba H. Rizvi

Syed Nurul H. Jafri

Syeda Saeeda Begum

Turfah Sobh

Zainab

Duʿāʾ al-Ḥujjah

اللهم كن لوليك الحجة بن الحسن صلواتك
عليه وعلى آبائه في هذه الساعة وفي كل
ساعة وليا وحافظا وقائدا وناصرا ودليلا
وعينا حتى تسكنه أرضك طوعا وتمتعه فيها طويلا

O God, be, for Your representative, the *Ḥujjat* (proof), son of al-Ḥasan, Your blessings be upon him and his forefathers, in this hour and in every hour: a guardian, a protector, a leader, a helper, a proof, and an eye - until You make him live on the Earth, in obedience (to You), and cause him to live in it for a long time.

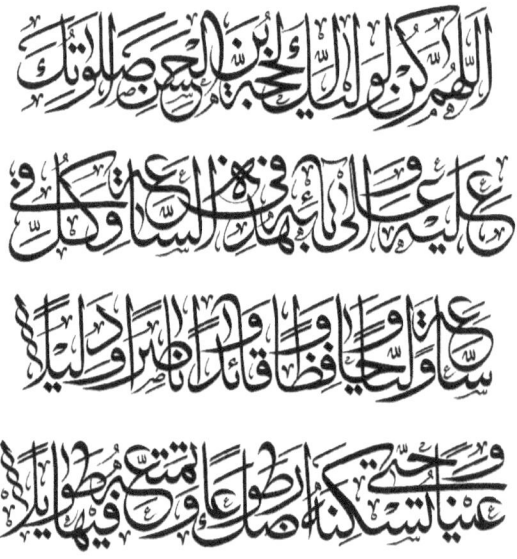

Terms of Respect

The following Arabic phrases have been used throughout this book in their respective places to show the reverence which the noble personalities deserve.

عزّ وجلّ

Used for God, meaning:
Exalted and Sublime (Perfect) is He

صلى الله عليه وآله

Used for Prophet Muḥammad, meaning:
Blessings from God be upon him and his family

عليه السلام

Used for a man (singular) of a high status, meaning:
Peace be upon him

عليها السلام

Used for a woman (singular) of a high status, meaning:
Peace be upon her

عليهما السلام

Used for men/women (dual) of a high status, meaning:
Peace be upon them both

عليهم السلام

Used for men and/or women (plural) of a high status, meaning:
Peace be upon them all

عجّل الله تعالى فرجه الشريف

Used for Imām Muḥammad al-Mahdī, meaning:
May God hasten his return

قدّس سرّه

Used for a deceased scholar, meaning:
May his resting [burial] place remain pure

Transliteration Table

The method of transliteration of Islamic terminology from the Arabic language has been carried out according to the standard transliteration table below.

ء	ʾ	ر	r	ف	f
ا	a	ز	z	ق	q
ب	b	س	s	ك	k
ت	t	ش	sh	ل	l
ث	th	ص	ṣ	م	m
ج	j	ض	ḍ	ن	n
ح	ḥ	ط	ṭ	و	w
خ	kh	ظ	ẓ	ه	h
د	d	ع	ʿ	ي	y
ذ	dh	غ	gh		
Long Vowels					
ا	ā	و	ū	ي	ī
Short Vowels					
ـَـ	a	ـُـ	u	ـِـ	i

Table of Contents

Preface

بسم الله الرحمن الرحيم

In the Name of God, the Beneficent, the Merciful

God ﷻ said:

﴿وَقالَ رَجُلٌ مُؤمِنٌ مِن آلِ فِرعَونَ يَكتُمُ إيمانَهُ أَتَقتُلونَ رَجُلًا أَن
يَقولَ رَبِّيَ اللَّهُ وَقَد جاءَكُم بِالبَيِّناتِ مِن رَبِّكُم ۖ وَإِن يَكُ كاذِبًا
فَعَلَيهِ كَذِبُهُ ۖ وَإِن يَكُ صادِقًا يُصِبكُم بَعضُ الَّذي يَعِدُكُم ۖ إِنَّ اللَّهَ
لا يَهدي مَن هُوَ مُسرِفٌ كَذّابٌ﴾

﴿*wa-qāla rajulun mu'minun min 'āli fir'awna yaktumu 'īmānahū 'a-taqtulūna rajulan 'an yaqūla rabbiya llāhu wa-qad jā'akum bi-l-bayyināti min rabbikum wa-'in yaku kādhiban fa-'alayhi kadhibuhū wa-'in yaku ṣādiqan yuṣibkum ba'ḍu lladhī ya'idukum 'inna llāha lā yahdī man huwa musrifun kadhdhāb*[un]﴾

﴿*Said a man of faith from Pharaoh's clan, who concealed his faith, 'Will you kill a man for saying, "My Lord is God," while he has already brought you manifest proofs from your Lord?*

Should he be lying, his falsehood will be to his own detriment; but if he is truthful, there shall visit you some of what he promises you. Indeed God does not guide someone who is a profligate, a liar﴾[1]

Praise be to God, Lord of all worlds, and may His peace and salutations be upon the best of His creations and last messenger Muḥammad and his immaculate progeny who are the bearers of His knowledge and preservers of His laws.

Islam comprises a belief system and a legislative body (the *Sharīʿa*). The belief system includes belief in God, his messengers, and the Day of Judgment. Furthermore, the Sharīʿa encompasses the divine laws that ensure, for mankind, the best quality of living and happiness in this world and the Hereafter.

The Islamic Sharīʿa is distinguished for its holistic nature and for providing solutions to all sorts of problems encountered by man in all aspects of his life. God ﷻ said:

[1] Sūrat Ghāfir, Verse 28.

﴿الْيَوْمَ أَكْمَلْتُ لَكُمْ دِينَكُمْ وَأَتْمَمْتُ عَلَيْكُمْ نِعْمَتِي وَرَضِيتُ لَكُمُ الْإِسْلَامَ دِينًا ۚ فَمَنِ اضْطُرَّ فِي مَخْمَصَةٍ غَيْرَ مُتَجَانِفٍ لِّإِثْمٍ ۙ فَإِنَّ اللَّهَ غَفُورٌ رَّحِيمٌ﴾

﴿l-yawma ʾakmaltu lakum dīnakum wa-ʾatmamtu ʿalaykum niʿmatī wa-raḍītu lakumu l-ʾislāma dīnan fa-mani ḍṭurra fī makhmaṣatin ghayra mutajānifin li-ʾithmin fa-ʾinna llāha ghafūrun raḥīmun﴾

﴿Today I have perfected your religion for you, and I have completed My blessing upon you, and I have approved Islam as your religion. But should anyone be compelled by hunger, without inclining to sin, then Allah is indeed Forgiving, Merciful﴾[2]

Nonetheless, there are subsidiary issues on which scholars have disagreed due to their disagreement on that which was narrated on behalf of the conveyer of the message, the Noble Prophet ﷺ, which caused discord in their outspoken opinions. Because truth emerges from studies, we have attempted – through this series of studies – to raise it as a subject matter

[2] Sūrat al-Māʾidah, Verse 3.

in hopes of it becoming a means to unify opinions and bridging perspectives in this field. Disagreement is not at the core of religion or its fundamentals; it would demand enmity and hatred. Instead, it is disagreement on the content of what was narrated on behalf of the Prophet ﷺ, which is minor compared to the many issues agreed upon amongst the Islamic sects.

Our leader in this path is His ﷻ saying:

﴿وَاعتَصِموا بِحَبلِ اللَّهِ جَميعًا وَلا تَفَرَّقوا ۚ وَاذكُروا نِعمَتَ اللَّهِ عَلَيكُم إِذ كُنتُم أَعداءً فَأَلَّفَ بَينَ قُلوبِكُم فَأَصبَحتُم بِنِعمَتِهِ إِخوانًا وَكُنتُم عَلىٰ شَفا حُفرَةٍ مِنَ النّارِ فَأَنقَذَكُم مِنها ۗ كَذٰلِكَ يُبَيِّنُ اللَّهُ لَكُم آياتِهِ لَعَلَّكُم تَهتَدونَ﴾

﴿wa-ʿtaṣimū bi-ḥabli llāhi jamīʿan wa-lā tafarraqū wa-dhkurū niʿmata llāhi ʿalaykum ʾidh kuntum ʾaʿdāʾan fa-ʾallafa bayna qulūbikum fa-ʾaṣbaḥtum bi-niʿmatihī ʾikhwānan wa-kuntum ʿalā shafā ḥufratin mina n-nāri fa-ʾanqadhakum minhā ka-dhālika yubayyinu llāhu lakum ʾāyātihī laʿallakum tahtadūn[a]﴾

⟨Hold fast, all together, to God's cord, and do not be divided [into sects]. And remember God's blessing upon you when you were enemies, then He brought your hearts together, so you became brothers with His blessing. And you were on the brink of a pit of Fire, whereat He saved you from it. Thus does God clarify His signs for you so that you may be guided⟩[3]

Jaʿfar Subḥānī

Qom, Institute of Imām Jaʿfar al-Ṣādiq 🌿

---

[3] Sūrat Āl ʿImrān, Verse 103.

Taqiyyah[4]: One of the Noble Islamic Concepts

Taqiyyah is considered one of the original Islamic concepts that are harmonized with the judgment of the intellect, the Islamic spirit, the leniency and flexibility of the sacred Sharīʿa, and the requirements of Islamic work. Moreover, it has been mentioned in the Noble Qurʾān, emphasized in the honorable Sunnah, and endorsed by Islamic scholars in terms of its legitimacy.

Indeed, the Shīʿas – due to the problematic circumstances inflicted upon them for a long historical period – were known for implementing Taqiyyah and resorting to it whenever the weight of oppression and injustice against them became heavier.

Ill-intentioned people such as oppressive rulers, dissenters, and extremists aimed at taking advantage of this issue by establishing false ideas and delusions and instilling them in people's minds while claiming that Taqiyyah – in Shīʿīsm – is a sort of hypocrisy, deception, and concealment which make of them a secret

---

[4] Taqiyyah means precautionary dissimulation or denial of religious belief and practice in the face of persecution.

organization whose purpose is to bypass Islam, distort its image and destroy its pillars.

Practicing Taqiyyah and being cautious with disclosing one's principles and thoughts do not mean that Shīʿas have secrets and mysteries which they exchange internally amongst themselves and exclude others from the opportunity of knowing them. It also does not mean that Shīʿas have aggressive intentions against Islam and its followers. It is, instead, all related to intellectual and political terrorism and the brutal crimes committed against them, which led them to concealment and caution in pursuit of safeguarding themselves and their reputation. Suppose we observe the Shīʿas during the mandates. They managed to have a margin of freedom. In that case, we will see how they took the initiative – proactively – to spread their thoughts and opinions and disseminate their principles and teachings. We will also see how they contributed – alongside their brothers from other schools and sects – to the establishment of an eternal Islamic civilization.

Whereby fairness calls for justifying the decisions of victims of suppression and tyranny in resorting to the shield of Taqiyyah in pursuit of safeguarding and protecting themselves from rampant evil and whereby an active conscience would call for consoling those oppressed people whose lives are at stake and who suffer from all sorts of pressure, force, restrictions, and hostility, none of the above took place. On the contrary, many Sunnīs – unfortunately – tended to overlook or support the murderers and denounce and defame the victims!

Lastly, we believe that adopting Taqiyyah is inevitable and that avoiding it entirely in all circumstances and ages is unrealistic and untrue. For, if you take a look at some nations that are ruled by suppressive and tyrannical regimes, you will find that this nation – which includes Sunnīs – avoids the declaration of their opinions and objectives out loud and remains quiet about the actions that are conducted in its midst in breach of Islamic provisions, out of fear from the brutality, murder, and harm that would be inflicted upon it if it decides to speak out against the will of the tyrants.

This humble publication will reveal that Taqiyyah is the fruit of the environment in which liberties have been confiscated. Suppose there must be any blame or criticism. In that case, it should be directed towards those who urged the oppressed to resort to Taqiyyah – and not towards the oppressed themselves.

Throughout this publication, it will become apparent to the reader that Taqiyyah is one of the Qur'ānic concepts that were mentioned more than once in the Noble Qur'ān, where there were clear implications to the circumstances in which the believer resorts to this lawful means in his life during harsh situations, in pursuit of safeguarding himself, his reputation and wealth, or the life of whom he is related to, their reputation and wealth.

It was used by the believer, who was related to Pharaoh, to protect the speaker from being murdered and tortured.[5]

---

[5] In reference to Sūrat al-Qaṣaṣ, Verse 20:

﴿وَجَاءَ رَجُلٌ مِنْ أَقْصَى الْمَدِينَةِ يَسْعَى قَالَ يَا مُوسَى إِنَّ الْمَلَأَ يَأْتَمِرُونَ بِكَ لِيَقْتُلُوكَ فَاخْرُجْ إِنِّي لَكَ مِنَ النَّاصِحِينَ﴾

⟨wa-jā'a rajulun min 'aqṣā l-madīnati yas'ā qāla yā-mūsā 'inna l-mala'a ya'tamirūna bika li-yaqtulūka fa-khruj 'innī laka mina n-nāṣiḥīna⟩

⟨And there came a man from the city outskirts, hurrying. He said, 'Moses! The elite are indeed conspiring to kill you. So leave. I am indeed your well-wisher.'⟩

And it was resorted to by ʿAmmār when he was captured and threatened with murder[6], in addition to other stances mentioned in the Qurʾān and the Sunnah. Therefore, we must learn about Taqiyyah regarding concepts (linguistically and contextually), history, objectives, proof, and limitations to avoid excess and deficiency regarding judgment and implementation.

The study of this topic requires the following clarifications in the next chapters.

---

[6] In reference to Sūrat al-Naḥl, Verse 106:

﴿مَن كَفَرَ بِاللَّهِ مِن بَعدِ إِيمانِهِ إِلّا مَن أُكرِهَ وَقَلبُهُ مُطمَئِنٌّ بِالإيمانِ وَلٰكِن مَن شَرَحَ بِالكُفرِ صَدرًا فَعَلَيهِم غَضَبٌ مِنَ اللَّهِ وَلَهُم عَذابٌ عَظيمٌ﴾

﴿man kafara bi-llāhi min baʿdi ʾīmānihī ʾillā man ʾukriha wa-qalbuhū muṭmaʾinnun bi-l-ʾīmāni wa-lākin man sharaḥa bi-l-kufri ṣadran fa-ʿalayhim ghaḍabun mina llāhi wa-lahum ʿadhābun ʿaẓīm[un]﴾

﴿Whoever renounces faith in God after [affirming] his faith — barring someone who is compelled while his heart is at rest in faith— but those who open up their breasts to unfaith, upon such shall be God's wrath, and there is a great punishment for them﴾

Taqiyyah in Terms of Linguistics

Taqiyyah is the source noun of the verb "ittaqā". The origin of "ittaqā" is: "iwtaqā إوتقى"; then the vowel "w" (و) was converted to a "ya'" (ي) due to the "kasra" preceding it. Alas, it was converted again to the letter "t" and merged with the letter before it. The word "ittiqā'" was mentioned repeatedly in the ḥadīth, amongst which is Imām 'Alī's ﷺ ḥadīth, "When the war got brutal, we would shield ourselves with the Messenger of God", that is, we resorted to him as our shield from the enemy."[7]

The word "ittaqā" was taken from "waqiya" (to protect) something, that is, to maintain it. God ﷻ said:

﴿فَوَقاهُ اللَّهُ سَيِّئاتِ ما مَكَروا﴾

﴿*fa-waqāhu llāhu sayyi'āti mā makarū*﴾

﴿*Then God saved him from their evil schemes*﴾[8]

---

[7] The finale: an object used for protection.

[8] Sūrat Ghāfir, Verse 45.

This means that He ﷻ protected him from them, whereby their schemes did not harm him.

Instead of the term "Taqiyyah", the term "tuqāt" may be used; for God ﷻ said:

﴿لا يَتَّخِذِ الْمُؤْمِنونَ الكافِرينَ أَولِياءَ مِن دونِ الْمُؤْمِنينَ ۖ وَمَن يَفعَل ذٰلِكَ فَلَيسَ مِنَ اللَّهِ في شَيءٍ إِلّا أَن تَتَّقوا مِنهُم تُقاةً﴾

﴿lā yattakhidhi l-mu'minūna l-kāfirīna 'awliyā'a min dūni l-mu'minīna wa-man yafʿal dhālika fa-laysa mina llāhi fī shay'in 'illā 'an tattaqū minhum tuqātan﴾

﴿The faithful should not take the faithless for allies instead of the faithful, and God will have nothing to do with those who do that, except when you are wary of them, out of caution﴾[9]

The majority read "tuqāt" except for Yaʿqūb, who read it as "Taqiyyah,"; and both are source nouns to the verb "ittaqa". "Tuqāt" originated from "waqiyya", then the "w" (و) was converted to the letter "t" as done with "tujat" (تجاة) and

[9] Sūrat Āl ʿImrān, Verse 28.

"tukat" (تكاة), and the "y" (ي) was converted to an "a" (ألف) due to its movement and due to the presence of a "fatha" before it. It is a source noun that rhymes with "fu'ila" (فُعِلَ), such as "tu'dad" and "tukhma".[10]

[10] Excerpt from the commentary of Aḥmad Muḥammad Shākir on the Center of Islamic Knowledge (Da'irat al-Ma'ārif al-Islāmiyyah): Vol. 5, p. 423.

Taqiyyah in Terms of Contextual Meaning

As defined by al-Sarkhasī, Taqiyyah is the act by which a person protects himself by what he reveals, even though he conceals otherwise.[11]

Ibn Ḥijr said: Taqiyyah is caution from disclosing what resides within a person – such as a belief or otherwise – to others.[12]

Ṣahib al-Manār defined it as that which is spoken or done in contradiction to righteousness in pursuit of safeguarding one's self from harm.[13]

As for Shaykh Muḥammad Abū Zahrāʾ, he defined it as the act by which a person conceals what he believes in averting harm.[14]

The third definition is more thorough than the fourth; as it includes belief and action, contrary to the fourth which is specific to belief.

---

[11] al-Sarkhasī, *al-Mabsūṭ*, Vol. 25, p. 4.

[12] al-ʿAsqalānī, Ibn Ḥajar, *Fath al-Bārī*: Vol. 12, p. 314, the edition of *al-Maktaba al-Salafiyya*.

[13] Rashīd b. ʿAlī Riḍā, *Tafsīr al-Manār*, Vol. 3, p. 280.

[14] Muḥammad Abū Zahrāʾ, *Imām Jaʿfar al-Ṣādiq* 🕮, p. 255.

Regarding the Shīʿa, Shaykh al-Mufīd defined the concept by saying: Taqiyyah is the concealment of righteousness and of one's belief in it, in addition to keeping quiet and abandoning disputes related to the actions of the objectors which inflict harm upon the religion or the worldly life.

Taqiyyah is mandatory once knowledge of harm or a strong likelihood thereof is established within a person. Therefore, when there is not any knowledge – or strong likelihood – established of the harm that would be inflicted upon disclosing righteousness, Taqiyyah ceases to be mandatory.[15]

Shaykh al-Ansāri defined it as the reservation about the harm inflicted by others by agreeing to what they say or do against the provisions of righteousness.[16]

---

[15] *Sharh 'Aqa'id al-Ṣadūq*, p. 66, the edition of Tabriz.

[16] Shaykh al-Ansāri, *Taqiyyah*, p. 37.

The History of Taqiyyah

It may be assumed that Taqiyyah is a concept that emerged during a specific period across human history; however, this is incorrect. For, the phenomenon of Taqiyyah is as old as the human being on this planet. It coexisted with the emergence of power amongst people, which led to the formation of the powerful and the weak, whereby the former suppressed the liberties of the latter and prohibited them from expressing themselves through speech or action.

Therefore, the appearance of Taqiyyah within the human community was an expression or a manifestation of the confiscation of rights and liberties and an indispensable weapon for the weak in pursuit of defending themselves, their dignity, and wealth.

Taqiyyah in the Time of the One to Whom God Spoke (referring to Prophet Mūsā عليه السلام)

The most obvious reference to this issue in the Noble Qur'ān is the believing man who was from Pharaoh's family clan, whereby God ﷻ said:

﴿وَقالَ رَجُلٌ مُؤمِنٌ مِن آلِ فِرعَونَ يَكتُمُ إيمانَهُ أَتَقتُلونَ رَجُلًا أَن يَقولَ رَبِّيَ اللَّهُ وَقَد جاءَكُم بِالبَيِّناتِ مِن رَبِّكُم ۖ وَإِن يَكُ كاذِبًا فَعَلَيهِ كَذِبُهُ ۖ وَإِن يَكُ صادِقًا يُصِبكُم بَعضُ الَّذي يَعِدُكُم ۖ إِنَّ اللَّهَ لا يَهدي مَن هُوَ مُسرِفٌ كَذّابٌ﴾

﴿wa-qāla rajulun mu'minun min 'āli fir'awna yaktumu 'īmānahū 'a-taqtulūna rajulan 'an yaqūla rabbiya llāhu wa-qad jā'akum bi-l-bayyināti min rabbikum wa-'in yaku kādhiban fa-'alayhi kadhibuhū wa-'in yaku ṣādiqan yuṣibkum ba'ḍu lladhī ya'idukum 'inna llāha lā yahdī man huwa musrifun kadhdhāb^un﴾

﴿Said a man of faith from Pharaoh's clan, who concealed his faith, 'Will you kill a man for saying, "My Lord is God," while he has already brought you manifest proofs from your Lord? Should he be lying, his falsehood will be to his own detriment; but if he is truthful, there shall visit you some of what he promises you. Indeed God does not guide someone who is a profligate, a liar'﴾[17]

---

[17] Sūrat Ghāfir, Verse 28.

The outcome was:

﴿فَوَقاهُ اللَّهُ سَيِّئَاتِ ما مَكَروا ۖ وَحاقَ بِآلِ فِرعَونَ سوءُ العَذابِ﴾

﴿*fa-waqāhu llāhu sayyi'āti mā makarū wa-ḥāqa bi-'āli fir'awna sū'u l-'adhābi*﴾

﴿*Then God saved him from their evil schemes, while a terrible punishment besieged Pharaoh's clan*﴾[18]

This was all since, through concealment, he managed to save the prophet of God from murder, as mentioned by God ﷻ:

﴿قالَ يا موسىٰ إِنَّ المَلَأَ يَأتَمِرونَ بِكَ لِيَقتُلوكَ فَاخرُج إِنّي لَكَ مِنَ النّاصِحينَ﴾

﴿*qāla yā-mūsā 'inna l-mala'a ya'tamirūna bika li-yaqtulūka fa-khruj 'innī laka mina n-nāṣiḥīna*﴾

﴿*He said, 'Moses! The elite are indeed conspiring to kill you. So leave. I am indeed your well-wisher.'*﴾[19]

---

[18] Sūrat Ghāfir, Verse 45.

[19] Sūrat al-Qaṣaṣ, Verse 20.

Al-Thaʿlabī narrated on behalf of al-Saddi and Muqātil that the believing man from Pharaoh's clan was Pharaoh's cousin about whom God ﷻ said:

﴿وَجاءَ رَجُلٌ مِن أَقصَى المَدينَةِ يَسعىٰ﴾

﴿wa-jāʾa rajulun min ʾaqṣā l-madīnati yasʿā﴾

﴿And there came a man from the city outskirts, hurrying﴾[20]

Others said he was Israeli and referred to the verse: *﴿Said a man of faith from Pharaoh's clan, who concealed his faith﴾*[21] There were different opinions regarding his name.

Ibn ʿAbbās and most scholars said that his name was Hizbil.

Wahab b. Manbah said that his name was Haziqal.

---

[20] Ibid.

[21] Sūrat Ghāfir, Verse 28.

Ibn Isḥāq said that it was Khabral.[22]

Taqiyyah in the Time of the Prophet ﷺ

Historical incidents indicate Taqiyyah's legitimacy during the time of the Prophet ﷺ, of which we will mention the following two examples.

1. God ﷻ says:

﴿مَن كَفَرَ بِاللَّهِ مِن بَعدِ إيمانِهِ إلّا مَن أُكرِهَ وَقَلبُهُ مُطمَئِنٌّ بِالإيمانِ﴾

﴿*man kafara bi-llāhi min baʿdi ʾīmānihī ʾillā man ʾukriha wa-qalbuhū muṭmaʾinnun bi-l-ʾīmāni*﴾

﴿*Whoever renounces faith in God after [affirming] his faith —barring someone who is compelled while his heart is at rest in faith*﴾[23]

The interpreters said that this verse was revealed to address a group of people who were forced to be disbelievers. They are ʿAmmār, his father,

[22] Aḥmad b. Muḥammad al-Thaʿlabī, *Tafsīr al-Thaʿlabī*, Vol. 8, p. 273.

[23] Sūrat al-Naḥl, Verse 106.

Yāsir, and his mother, Sumayyah. His parents were murdered after they refused to show disbelief and dishonor the Prophet ﷺ; meanwhile, 'Ammār gave them what they wanted, so they set him free. He then told the Prophet, and the incident went viral among Muslims. Some people said: 'Ammār has become a disbeliever, to which the Messenger of God ﷺ responded, "No, 'Ammār is full of faith – from head to toe; and faith has been integrated within his flesh and blood."

Thereupon, the verse mentioned above descended. 'Ammār used to cry, and the Messenger of God ﷺ would wipe away his tears and say, "If they come to you again, say exactly what you have said before."[24]

2. Ibn Abī Shabība narrated, "on behalf of al-Ḥasan, that Mūsaylima – the liar – took two of the Prophet's companions and said to one of them:

Do you witness that Muḥammad is the Messenger of God? He said: yes, he said: Do you

---

[24] Ṭabrisī, Shaykh Faḍl b. Ḥasan, *Majma' al-Bayān fī Tafsīr al-Qur'ān*, Vol. 3, p. 388.

witness that I am the Messenger of God? He said: yes. Then he called the other person and asked him: Do you witness that Muḥammad is the Messenger of God? He said: yes. So he asked him: Do you witness I am God's Messenger? He said: I am deaf. He asked him three times to which he gave the same response. Thus, he struck his neck." The Messenger of God ﷺ was informed about this incident. He said: "As for the murdered person, he carried on with honesty and conviction and acted upon virtue. Congratulations to him!"

As for the other person, he acted per God's ﷻ permission and is not held accountable for anything.[25]

Taqiyyah after the Messenger of God ﷺ

The Umayyads took advantage of destiny and fate to emphasize that everything in the Islamic

---

[25] Musnad Ibn Shība, Vol. 12, p. 358, the edition of al-Salafiyya; al-Tibyan, Vol. 2, p. 453, al-Tousi commented on the narration by saying: Based on that, Taqiyyah is permissible and speaking the truth is a virtue. Our narrations seem to indicate that it is mandatory and acting otherwise is wrongdoing. You will be presented later with its five divisions.

community had taken place upon God's decree and destiny and that no one had any choice or right to object to the matter. Accordingly, the widespread poverty amongst the Muslims was decreed by God ﷻ; and the luxurious life enjoyed by the Umayyads and their oppression against Muslims was also decreed by God ﷻ.

Whereas that claim was contradictory to the necessity of religion and the mission of the prophets, some stood up against that idea; At the same time, many remained silent out of fear of the Umayyad's brutality. Thus, they concealed their beliefs and adopted Taqiyyah.

Ibn Saʿd narrates, on behalf of al-Ḥasan al-Baṣri, that he used to disagree with the Umayyads' understanding of destiny. Then, when some of his friends warned him of the sultan, he promised not to disagree with them again.

Ibn Saʿd narrated in his '*Tabaqāt*', on behalf of Ayyūb, that he said: I debated, several times, with al-Ḥasan over the topic of destiny until I frightened him from the sultan, to which he responded that he would never debate over it again.[26]

Al-Ma'mūn wrote to Isḥāq b. Ibrāhīm – the head of police in Baghdad then – and asked him to send the following seven narrators:

1. Muḥammad b. Sa'd Katib al-Waqidi
2. Abū Muslim, Mustamli Yazīd b. Hārūn
3. Yaḥyā b. Mu'īn
4. Zuhayr b. Harb Abū Khuthayma
5. Ismā'īl b. Dāwūd
6. Ismā'īl b. Abī Mas'ud
7. Aḥmad b. al-Duraqi.

Al-Ma'mūn tested them and asked them about the creation of the Qur'ān, to which they all responded that the Qur'ān was created. So, he sent them to the city of al-Salām; and Isḥāq b.

---

[26] Ibn Sa'd, Kitāb aṭ-Tabaqāt al-Kabīr, Vol. 7, p. 167, Beirut edition.

Ibrāhīm invited them over to his place and exposed them and their responses in front of the narrating scholars and Shaykhs; thus, they confirmed what they had said to al-Ma'mūn previously, so he set them free. Isḥāq b. Ibrāhīm did so at the command of al-Ma'mūn.

It is mentioned that the popular opinion amongst the narrators was that the Qur'ān was not created. However, they adopted Taqiyyah and admitted to the creationism of the Qur'ān. This is the same sort of Taqiyyah adopted by the Shī'as, and the narrators practiced it during the mandate of al-Ma'mūn.

There is another letter by al-Ma'mūn to Isḥāq b. Ibrāhīm – the head of police, said: The commander of the faithful finds the person who utters such words (that the Qur'ān is not created) to be lacking in religion and faith.

Once Isḥāq b. Ibrāhīm received the letter, he summoned a group of twenty-six narrators and read it to them twice until they fully grasped it. Then, he invited them – one by one – and they all admitted that the Qur'ān was created except for the following four people:

1. Aḥmad b. Ḥanbal

2. Sajada

3. al-Qawārīrī

4. Muḥammad b. Nūḥ al-Madrub.

Isḥāq b. Ibrāhīm ordered them to have them tied to iron shackles. The next day, he summoned them all, and they were brought in with shackles. He re-administered the question, to which Sajada responded that the Qur'ān was created, so he was set free. Meanwhile, the others insisted on their stances.

The following day, he summoned them again and repeated the question. Al-Qawārīrī responded that the Qur'ān was created, upon which he was set free. Meanwhile, Aḥmad b. Ḥ and Muḥammad b. Nūḥ insisted on their stances and did not retract their statements. So, they were all tied to iron shackles and sent to Ṭarṭūs with a report that confirmed their test results.

When the retractors were confronted with the objection, they justified their stances by referring to 'Ammār b. Yāsir who was forced to claim polytheism while his heart was filled with faith.[27]

This indicates that Taqiyyah is a legitimate principle Muslims adopt whenever they feel weak in front of an oppressive government.

Therefore, accusing Shī'as of its unique adoption of Taqiyyah contradicts the Noble Qur'ān, the Prophetic Sunnah, and the practice of Muslims throughout history.

Taqiyyah is the weapon of the weak. It is the weapon of those whose rights and liberties have been confiscated by a controlling and oppressive government that does not show any sort of flexibility in its stances. Moreover, it is the judgment of reason; for it is a form of self-defense and safeguarding all that is valuable by showing agreement through speech and action until harm is avoided, after which a person returns to his original state.

---

[27] Muḥammad al-Ṭabarī, *Tārīkh al-Ṭabarī*, Vol. 7, p. 197, Hawadith of the year 218 AH.

Such practice cannot be specific or exclusive to only one group.

The Shīʿas' Ordeal During the Mandates of the Umayyads and ʿAbbāsids

The Shīʿas were well known for Taqiyyah more than other groups; for they – more than others – were exposed to pressure, confiscation of liberties at the slightest accusation, displacement, and murder everywhere they went.

What led the Shīʿas, expressly – amongst their religious brothers – to adopt Taqiyyah was their fear of the oppressive governments. Had there not been any pressure against the Shīʿas during the past centuries – from the Umayyads' mandate until the ʿAbbāsids and then the Ottomans – and had their countries and homes not been soaked in their blood – and history is the best witness thereof – then it would have been likely for the Shīʿas to forget all about Taqiyyah and eliminate it from their lives. However, unfortunately, many of their brothers were obedient tools at the disposal of the Umayyads and ʿAbbāsids, who perceived the Shīʿa school as a threat to their power and positions. They used to turn the Sunnīs against the Shīʿas, which caused them to murder, persecute and brutalize them. Thereupon, due to those difficult circumstances, the Shīʿas – as any reasonable person – did not have a resort to turn to except for Taqiyyah or abandon the sacred principles more precious to them than their own lives and wealth.

The testaments for that are countless; nonetheless, we will present a brief summary: One of these is what Muʿāwīya b. Abī Sufyān wrote in regards to legitimizing the murder of Shīʿas wherever they were and regardless of their condition. Below you can find the script that was mentioned in the references concerning this incident so that you can realize the Shīʿas' ordeal:

The Shīʿas' Ordeal during the Umayyad Mandate

Abū al-Ḥasan ʿAlī b. Muḥammad b. Abī Sayf al-Madāʾinī narrated in his book '*al-Aḥdāth*' that Muʿāwīya b. Abī Sufyān wrote one copy to his employees after the year of "al-jamāʿa": I absolve myself from anyone who speaks of the virtues of Abū Turāb ﷺ and his household. Thereupon, the speakers started to curse and disavow Imām ʿAlī ﷺ and his household in every city and platform. The most severely afflicted people back then were the people of Kūfa due to the many Shīʿas residing therein. So, Muʿāwīya b. Abī Sufyān assigned Zīyād b. Sumayyah as a ruler of Kūfa - and later on al-Basra as well. He used to follow up closely with the Shīʿas and was knowledgeable of their conditions; for he was one of them during the days of Imām ʿAlī ﷺ. Zīyād killed them wherever he found them, terrorized them, severed their arms and legs, blinded their eyes, crucified them on the branches of palm trees, and expelled and banished them from Iraq until none of them was left there. Muʿāwīya b. Abī Sufyān wrote to his employees all across the country, ordering them not to accept testimony from any of Imām ʿAlī's ﷺ followers.

Then he wrote one copy to his employees in all the countries:

Look for those who were proven to have loved Imām ʿAlī ﷺ and his household, remove them from all the public administrative positions, condemn any provision for them, and ruin their sustenance. He attached the letter with another copy that said: Whomever you accuse of following these people, torment him and destroy his home. These afflictions peaked in Iraq, especially in Kufa, to the extent that a man from the followers of Imām ʿAlī ؑ would welcome – in his home – someone who trusted him. This person would enter his house and disclose his secrets while being fearful of his servant and slave. He would not speak to him until the other would solemnly swear that he would keep that secret.

Ibn Abī Hadid added: The situation remained as is up until the death of Imām al-Ḥusayn b. ʿAlī ؑ, upon which the afflictions increased, and no one of this sort remained unless he was scared for his life or fleeing across the globe.

Then, things got worse after the murder of Imām al-Ḥusayn ؑ and the rise of ʿAbdul Mālik b. Marwān as the new caliph. He was even harsher with the Shīʿas. He assigned al-Ḥajjāj b. Yūsuf as the governor, and the people known for their worship, virtue, and religion, got close to him by showing their hatred towards Imām ʿAlī ؑ and following his enemies – and those who claimed to be his enemies. They spoke abundantly of their merits, achievements, and

virtues, and they spoke hatefully against Imām
'Alī 🕊. They spoke of his faults, slandered him,
and mentioned him with contempt. One
person even approached al-Ḥajjāj - it was said
that he was the grandfather of al-Asma'ī 'Abdul
Mālik b. Qarib – and cried: O' prince, my
parents dishonored me and named me 'Alī.
Thus, I am deprived and miserable and in dire
need of connecting with the prince. Al-Ḥajjāj,
then, laughed with him and said: Due to your
delightful pleading, I will bestow upon you the
following position.[28]

The Umayyad party continued its terrorism and
bloodbaths throughout its entire mandate.
History recorded other incidents that manifest
the worst forms of terror and undervaluing of
righteousness and justice during the mandate of
'Abdul Mālik b. Marwān and his killing of Sa'īd
b. Jubayr. 'Abdul Mālik b. Marwān wrote a
letter in which he assigned Khālid b. 'Abd Allāh
al-Qasri as a governor and said:

Moreover, I have assigned Khālid b. 'Abd Allāh
al-Qasri as your governor; therefore, follow him

---

28 Ibn Abī l-Ḥadīd, *Sharḥ Nahj al-Balāgha*, Vol. 11, p. 44-46.

and abide by his word. Do not allow yourself to have its way with you; for its punishment will be murder and nothing else. I disavow any man who provides shelter for Saʿīd b. Jubayr. Peace. Then, Khālid looked at them and said: I swear by He to whom we swear and towards whom we perform a pilgrimage that if I find him in a person's house, I will kill that person, destroy his house, and the houses of his neighbors and violate all that is sacred to him. I will give you three days from now before I execute my promise.[29]

Then, Saʿīd b. Jubayr – who was one of the pioneer followers of the Prophet's household – was arrested and handed to al-Ḥajjāj, who killed him. Al-Ḥajjāj was the most notorious butcher in Islamic history, who murdered tens of thousands of objectors against the government.

Imām Muḥammad al-Bāqir عليه السلام described to some of his companions his environment and the community in which he lived; he said: "O' companion, we have endured Quraysh's repression and protest against us; and our

[29] *al-Imāmah wa al-Siyāsah*, Vol. 2, p. 47, printed in Egypt.

followers and lovers suffered a lot from people...." Then, he said: "We – the household of the Prophet – continue to be humiliated and oppressed, expelled and subjugated, deprived and murdered. We feel unsafe and scared for our lives and the lives of our followers. The liars and ungrateful have found a way to their masters and to the wicked agents and judges in every city by inventing lies and narrating – on our behalf – what we have not said or done in pursuit of turning people's hearts against us. This reached its peak during the mandate of Muʿāwiya b. Abī Sufyān after the death of Imām al-Ḥasan 🕮, upon which our followers were murdered all across the country, and arms and legs were severed upon mere suspicion. All who were remembered for their love for us were imprisoned, robbed of their wealth, or had their homes destroyed. The afflictions kept growing up until the mandate of ʿUbayd Allāh b. Zīyād, the murderer of Imām al-Ḥusayn 🕮. Then, al-Hajjaj came and killed them all upon accusation and suspicion, to the extent that a man – back then – preferred to be called a disbeliever or a heretic rather than a follower of Imām ʿAlī 🕮.[30]

---

[30] Ibn Abī l-Ḥadīd, *Sharḥ Nahj al-Balāgha*, Vol. 11, p. 43-44.

The Ordeal of the Shīʿas during the ʿAbbāsid Mandate

Akin to the Umayyad authority, the ʿAbbāsid authority executed a policy of tyranny, murder, and displacement. It was even more tyrannical and tormenting, as indicated by Abū al-Faraj al-Asfahani when he spoke of al-Mutawakkil:

Al-Mutawakkil was brutal with the relatives of Abī Ṭālib. He was severely harsh with them, extremely loathsome and hateful of them, and suspicious and accusatory against them. He assigned, over Madīnah and Makkah, ʿUmar b. al-Faraj al-Rakhji forbade the relatives of Abī Ṭālib to ask for people's support and prohibited the people from assisting with any of them. Whenever he heard of anyone supporting them – with the most trivial things – he would sentence him with a penalty and a fine. Each group of women who were followers of Imām ʿAlī عليه السلام would have only one garment, which they would share so that they would – one after the other – pray, then patch it and sit in their knitting space bare and naked.[31]

[31] Abū l-Faraj al-Isfahānī, *Maqātil al-Ṭālibiyyīn*, p. 395-396.

It was the desire of the prince of believers, al-Mutawakkil, to have the female followers of Imām ʿAlī ﷺ bound naked to their homes – sharing a patched garment at prayer time – while the debauched whores walk around boastfully in jewelry and brocade amongst the handmaids and slaves. Al-Rashīd sent someone to strip the daughters of the Messenger from their clothes; whereas al-Mutawakkil was more restrictive and harsh with them to the extent that he led them towards nudity. That is how the philosophies and approaches develop with time at the hands of the Arabs of Quraysh – sons of the glorious and the noble!

The Shīʿas separated from each other during the mandate of al-Mutawakkil. Some decided to hide and passed away in that condition, such as Aḥmad b. ʿĪsā al-Ḥusayn and ʿAbd Allāh b. Mūsā al-Ḥusayn. Some revolted against tyranny and oppression such as Muḥammad b. Saleh and Muḥammad b. Jaʿfar.

It was not enough for al-Mutawakkil to tyrannize the living, so he attacked the graves and destroyed the grave of Imām al-Ḥusayn ﷺ and all the surrounding homes and residences.

He also prohibited people from visiting him, and his caller announced that whoever was found to be visiting the grave of Imām al-Ḥusayn ﷺ would be imprisoned in the underground prison. A poet said in this regard:

The Umayyad authority has risen;

The son of its Prophet's daughter was oppressively murdered.

The sons of their fathers committed a similar act;

For you can see his grave utterly destroyed.

They were regretful for not following him when he was murdered;

So they followed him in his ruins.[32]

Taqiyyah was rising, at times, amongst Shīʿas and, at other times, declining based on the gravity of the pressure endured. For, there was a vast difference between the mandate of al-Ma'mūn who allowed people to praise Ahl al-

---

[32] *al-Shīʿa wal-Ḥakīmūn*, p. 169-170.

Bayt عليهم السلام and honored the followers of Imām ʿAlī عليه السلام and the mandate of al-Mutawakkil who used to cut the tongue of anyone who speaks of their virtues.

A good example is Ibn Sukayt, one of the renowned literary figures during the time of al-Mutawakkil. The former had chosen him as a teacher for his sons. So, one day he asked him: "Who is dearer to your heart, my two sons of al-Ḥasan and al-Ḥusayn? Ibn Sukayt said: By God, Qanbar – the servant of ʿAlī عليه السلام – is better than you and your two sons. Then, al-Mutawakkil said: Cut off his tongue; so they did, upon which he died. When Ibn Sukayt died, al-Mutawakkil gave his son, Yūsuf, ten thousand Dirhams and said: This is the atonement for your father's killing!"[33]

Ibn al-Rumi, the brilliant poet, mentions in his eulogy for Yaḥyā b. ʿUmar b. al-Ḥusayn b. ʿAlī Zayd b. ʿAlī:

---

[33] Ibn Khallikān, *Wafayāt al-Aʿyān*, Vol. 3, p. 33.

Shams ad-Dīn adh-Dhahabī, *Siyār Aʿlām al-Nubalāʾ*, Vol. 12, p. 16.

"Has it become a norm that, every while, the Prophet Muḥammad has a relative who is murdered and drenched in his blood?

O' sons of the Chosen One, how many people have oppressed you! May your afflictions soon be relieved!

Would the lanterns of the sky glow after the martyrdom of al-Ḥusayn?"[34]

The 'Abbāsids were more hateful and loathsome of the followers of Imām 'Alī ﷺ than the Umayyads; for, they committed heinous acts of murder, burning, persecution, and torture against them. For, al-Manṣūr would receive, from Madīnah, all those who were followers of Imām 'Alī ﷺ tied up in chains and shackles. Once they arrived, he would detain them in dark prison cells where they would not know the days from the nights. If any of them died, he would be left in there with them; finally, he would order to destroy the prison while they were in it. In this regard, one of the Shī'a poets said:

---

[34] Ibn al-Rūmī, *Dīwān Ibn al-Rūmī*, Vol. 2, p. 243.

By God, what the Umayyads have done to them was one-tenth of what was perpetrated against them by the ʿAbbāsids.

Another poet said:

"I wish that the oppression committed against us by the sons of Marwān had been prolonged, and I wish that the justice of the sons of ʿAbbās goes to Hellfire."[35]

Abū Firās said:

"The sons of war did not get to them – though be the crimes grand;

Yet the ones perpetrated by you did."

Al-Sharīf al-Raḍī said:

"The former's actions – though grave – were not as heinous as those of the latter."

Shaykh Muḥammad b. Ḥasan Ṭūsī, who lived during the progressive stages of the ʿAbbāsid

---

[35] The poem is by Abī ʿAṭā' al-Sindī.

caliphate, said as he described the Shīʿas' condition:

"No group or sect was exposed to the afflictions endured by Shīʿas. For, we almost cannot identify a period during which the Shīʿas were safe and needless of Taqiyyah, nor a condition where they were not targeted by the sultan's extremism, tendencies, and perversion."[36]

This is a brief overview of the Shīʿas' ordeals during the ʿAbbāsid period, which continued at the same pace during later periods such as the Ayyūbid and Ottoman mandates.

The Shīʿas' Ordeal during the Ayyūbid and Ottoman Mandates

Once Salāḥ al-Dīn al-Ayyūbi took power from the Fatimids, he discharged the Shīʿa judges and replaced them with Shāfiʿī judges. He also nullified and removed the phrase "Hasten towards the best of actions". People claimed the Mālikī and Shāfiʿī doctrines, and the Shīʿa sect began to disappear until it was utterly forgotten

[36] Ṭūsī, Shaykh Muḥammad b. Ḥasan, *Talkhīṣ al-Shāfī*, Vol. 2, p. 59.

in Egypt. He used to force people to adopt the Sunnī doctrine and the Ashʿarīyah belief system, and whoever chose otherwise would have his neck struck. He also ordered people to reject the testimony, speech, and tutoring of anyone who does not follow one of the four Sunnī schools. Al-Khafajī said, in his book "Al-Azhar in a Thousand Years": The Ayyūbids overdid themselves by eliminating any trace of Shīʿas.

As for the Ottoman era, Sultan Salīm became the leader of the Sunnīs and acquired a ruling from wicked Shaykhs that said that Shīʿas had transgressed religion and, therefore, it became mandatory to kill them. Thus, he ordered the killing everyone known for being a Shīʿa within his country.

Upon that command, forty thousand Shīʿas people were murdered in Anadul one – some say seventy thousand – for the sole reason of being Shīʿas. Sayyid Sharaf al-Dīn mentioned in his "al-Fusul al-Arbaʿa" that Shaykh Nūḥ al-Ḥanafi established a ruling which considered the Shīʿas to be disbelievers and mandated their murder. Thus, upon this ruling, tens of thousands of Shīʿas from Ḥalab (Aleppo) were killed until there was not any Shīʿa left therein – provided that Shīʿīsm was embedded and widespread in Ḥalab since it was the capital of the Ḥamdanid state. A long time ago, many scholars and jurisprudential pioneers rose in Ḥalab, such as Banī Zuhra, Al Abī Jarada, and others who were mentioned in biography books and translations, especially the book "*ʿĀmal al-ʿĀmil*".[37]

The Ottomans killed al-Shahīd al-Thānī, known for his bounties, God-weariness, and respectable scholastic books, some of which are still being taught - today - in the universities of Najaf and Qom. The governor of Akka, known as al-Jazzār (the butcher), did in Jabal ʿĀmil what al-Ḥajjāj did in Iraq.

Al-Jazzār confiscated the wealth and libraries of those who lived in Jabal ʿĀmil. The library of Al-Khatoun contained five thousand books, and the ovens of Akka kept burning the books of Jabal ʿĀmil for a whole week. None managed to evade al-Jazzār's oppression save those who

---

[37] *al-Fuṣūl al-Arbaʿah*, p. 206, ch. 9.

Ghaniyyat al-Nuzūʿ, p. 11, Introduction.

managed to flee. In his time, the scholars of Jabal ʿĀmil were displaced and fled in all directions. One of them was the Shīʿa poet, Ibrāhīm Yaḥyā, who fled to Damascus while carrying anguish, heartbreak, and awful memories of the heinous crimes committed by al-Jazzār. These memories never parted him; for he eye-witnessed and described them in heartbreaking poems, of which was a long poem where he said:

It saddens us to leave while our Egypt remains a prize and spoils chosen by Pharaoh.

The homes of people of justice are empty, while the oppressive people have a wide and extensive army.

This briefly overviews the Shīʿas' ordeals during the Ottoman period. Despite the widespread freedom in our current times, Shīʿas still practice Taqiyyah in most countries. Otherwise, they would suffer many restrictions.

ʿAllāmah Sayyid Hibat al-Dīn al-Shahrastānī says: Taqiyyah is the practice of every weak person whose freedom has been stolen. Shīʿas were famous for Taqiyyah because they were more afflicted with continuous pressure than others. They were robbed of their freedom during the entire Umayyad mandate, the entire 'Abbāsid mandate, and most of the Ottoman mandate. That is why they resorted to Taqiyyah more than others. Whereby Shī'as disagreed with other sects in regards to a significant part of their beliefs in the origins of religion and many jurisprudential rulings, and whereby disagreement attracts surveillance – as proved by experience, it was necessary for the Shī'as of the Imāms of Ahl al-Bayt ﷺ – in many situations – to conceal what is specific to them in terms of practice, beliefs, rulings, books or otherwise. Through this concealment, the Shī'as aim at safeguarding one's life and valuables, in addition to preserving the amiability and brotherhood amongst their other Muslim brothers, so that they all remain under the umbrella of obedience and the disbelievers do not sense any discord within the Islamic community which leads them to widen such discord within the nation of Muḥammad ﷺ.

For these noble purposes, Shī'as exercised Taqiyyah. They preserved their accord with other sects outwardly, following – thereby – the footsteps of the Imāms who belonged to the progeny of Prophet Muḥammad ﷺ and their strict rulings on the mandatory nature of Taqiyyah such as: "Taqiyyah is my religion and my fathers'." God's religion carried on through the practice of Taqiyyah by those who were robbed of their freedom. This was indicated in the verses of the Noble Qur'ān[38].

It was narrated that Imām Jaʿfar al-Ṣādiq عليه السلام said in *al-Athar al-Sahīh*, "Taqiyyah is my religion and my fathers'."

Taqiyyah was the practice of Ahl al-Bayt عليهم السلام in pursuit of protecting themselves and their followers from harm, suspending bloodshed in their midst, reforming the condition of Muslims, unifying their word, and bringing together their divisions. Taqiyyah remains an attribute that famously belongs to the Imāmate Shīʿas rather than other sects and nations. Every person who senses danger upon himself or his wealth due to disseminating his beliefs or being

---

[38] Sūrat Ghāfir, Verse 28 and Sūrat al-Naḥl, Verse 106. Each verse/translation/transliteration were previously provided.

explicit about them must be discreet and cautious of dangerous places. The primordial nature of reason demands such practice.

It is well-known that the Shīʿas and their Imāms عليهم السلام were exposed to severe afflictions and restrictions upon their liberties during all the mandates, unlike any other sect or nation. Accordingly, in most mandates, they had to practice Taqiyyah while interacting with dissenting counterparts, forsake any debate, and conceal their beliefs and practices that were exclusively theirs due to the harm they may cause them.

That is why they were exclusively famous for practicing Taqiyyah[39].

Conclusion

In conclusion, the Shīʿa community encountered heinous massacres by oppressive governments. Thousands were killed, and those who remained alive were exposed to torture, terrorism, and intimidation. Truth be told:

---

[39] *al-Mushīd Magazine*, Vol. 3, p. 252 – 253, commentaries of the first essays on p. 96.

incredibly, this sect still has people who have survived despite all the oppression and massive killing. The most fantastic thing is that this sect has only grown stronger and larger and has established countries and developed civilizations and given rise to many scholars and intellectuals.

Therefore, if a Sunnī brother considers Taqiyyah a prohibited act, he should work on alleviating the pressure endured by his Shīʿa brother and refrain from restricting his freedom, which Islam allows Muslims. He must excuse him for his beliefs and practices, just like he excused many others who violated the Noble Qur'ān and Sunnah, shed blood, and robbed the country. Shīʿas are people who share with him the same religion and agree with him on many of his beliefs. And if Muʿāwīya b. Abī Sufyān and his household and the ʿAbbāsids were all Mujtahids in their oppression and bloodshed of their objectors, then what prevents him from excusing the Shīʿas and considering them Mujtahids as well?

If they say – and that is the significant part – that waging war against Imām ʿAlī ﷺ does not affect the justice of those dissenters and rebels that were pioneered by Ṭalha, Zubayr and ʿĀʾisha – the mother of believers, and that stirring up discord in Siffīn – which ended up in the murder of many companions and followers and the bloodshed of thousands of Iraqis and Syrians – does not reduce any of the warriors' God-weariness, and that due to being Mujtahids they are excused and deserve the reward of the Mujtahid who misses, why then does he not treat Shīʿas based on the same concepts and perceive them as being deserving of pardon – nay of reward?

The Purpose of Legislating Taqiyyah

The purpose of Taqiyyah is preserving one's self, honor, and wealth in compelling circumstances in which a believer cannot disclose his true stance out of fear of the harm and damage that would result thereof at the hands of oppressive forces that commit terrorism, displacement and exile, murder and torture, confiscation of wealth and deprivation of due rights. Thereupon, this believer – who claims himself righteous – finds it inevitable to conceal his beliefs and pretend to hold the beliefs which agree with the ruler's wishes and ways in pursuit of safeguarding himself from persecuting, torture, and murder until God ﷻ brings about a new situation.

Taqiyyah is the weapon of the weak vis-à-vis the brute and oppressive. It is the weapon of those afflicted with people who do not respect their blood, honor, or property solely to disagree with them on some principles and thoughts.

Taqiyyah is practiced by those who live in an environment where their opinions, beliefs, and freedom of speech and action are confiscated such that the only way for them to survive is to remain quiet – unwillingly – or speak out what agrees with the authority in power, in terms of wishes and thoughts. A person may also resort to it to save a persecuted person in need or vulnerable people who are utterly powerless. This person may, in this case, pretend to be working to the benefit of the oppressive government to fulfill his pursuits, as was the case of the believer who belonged to Pharaoh's family, which was mentioned in the Noble Qur'ān.

Most of those who condemn Taqiyyah and those who practice it assume its purpose lies in establishing secret groups that aim at causing destruction and sabotage – for which the Esoteric (*Batiniyya*) and Atheist private parties are known. This incorrect assumption was adopted, out of ignorance or on purpose, without basing it on any proof or valid evidence. For, their judgment was not even close to the line of the reason we have provided. Had these oppressed believers not been afflicted with compelling circumstances and abusive rulings, they would not have resorted to Taqiyyah, nor would they have endured the burden of concealing their beliefs; in fact, they would have called people towards these beliefs explicitly without any hesitation.

Where does a defensive act stand when compared to the actions committed by secretive groups that aim at overthrowing a government and taking charge? All these are carefully-schemed plans aimed at nefarious purposes.

Those people carry the slogan "the ends justify the means", which means that every illegal or reasonably horrible thing becomes plausible – for them – to reach disastrous pursuits.

Comparing – and associating – between these people and those who take up Taqiyyah as a shield and a defensive weapon to safeguard themselves from another's evil, so that he would not be killed or uprooted, and so that his house and property would not get robbed - until God brings about another condition – seems to be like comparing between two utterly different things.

Muslims who lived in the former Soviet Union had encountered unthinkable calamities and afflictions which cannot be tolerated even by mere thought. During their mandate over Islamic areas, the communists turned against the Muslims. They confiscated their wealth, property, homes, mosques, and schools; they also burned down their libraries and killed many of them brutally and atrociously, leaving none of them except for those who protected themselves by pretending to be flexible, concealing their religious ceremonies and establishing their prayers at home until God ﷻ saved them by demolishing that disbelieving power. Muslims, then, rose again, regained possession over their lands and homes, and gradually retrieved their glory and honor. All this is the fruit of Taqiyyah's legitimate practice, which God ﷻ allowed for his servants through his bounties and generosity with the vulnerable.

Suppose this is the meaning and concept of Taqiyyah, and those were its purpose and objectives. In that case, it is a natural and innate response. Man's reason and heart lead him towards Taqiyyah, and his primordial nature invites him to that. That is why it is the haven for anyone afflicted by kings and rulers who do not respect anything but their own opinion, idea, aspirations, and power and do not hesitate to torture every dissenting objector without differentiating between a Muslim – Shīʿa or Sunnī – and otherwise. Herein lies the purpose of Taqiyyah and the depth of its benefits.

We will study its proof from the Noble Qurʾān and the Sunnah to support this dynamic principle.

Taqiyyah in the Beloved Qur'ān

Taqiyyah was legislated by Qur'ānic texts, whereby it was mentioned in several noble verses,[40] which we will present in the following pages.

The First Verse:

﴿مَن كَفَرَ بِاللَّهِ مِن بَعدِ إِيمانِهِ إِلّا مَن أُكرِهَ وَقَلبُهُ مُطمَئِنٌّ بِالإِيمانِ وَلٰكِن مَن شَرَحَ بِالكُفرِ صَدرًا فَعَلَيهِم غَضَبٌ مِنَ اللَّهِ وَلَهُم عَذابٌ عَظيمٌ﴾

﴾man kafara bi-llāhi min ba'di 'īmānihī 'illā man 'ukriha wa-qalbuhū muṭma'innun bi-l-'īmāni wa-lākin man sharaḥa bi-l-kufri ṣadran fa-'alayhim ghaḍabun mina llāhi wa-lahum 'adhābun 'aẓīm[un]*﴿*

﴾Whoever renounces faith in God after [affirming] his faith —barring someone who is compelled while his heart is at rest in faith— but those who open up their breasts to unfaith,

---

40 Sūrat Ghāfir, Verses 28 and 45; Sūrat al-Qaṣaṣ, Verse 20. Each verse/translation/transliteration were previously provided.

Other verses will soon be mentioned.

upon such shall be God's wrath, and there is a great punishment for them﴾[41]

We can see that God ﷻ permits the display of disbelief – when forced and playing with disbelievers out of fear of them – on the condition that the heart is filled with faith. Many old and contemporary interpreters declared this interpretation. We will present the words of some in order to avoid lengthiness, and whoever wants further information can review the different exegesis books:

1. Al-Ṭabrasi said: This verse addressed a group of people who were forced to disbelieve, and they were 'Ammār, his father Yāsir, and his mother, Sumayyah. The parents were killed since they refused to manifest disbelief and affect the Prophet ﷺ. As for 'Ammār, he gave them what they wanted, so they set him free. Then, 'Ammār told the Messenger of God ﷺ, and the incident became widespread among Muslims. Some people said: 'Ammār disbelieved, to which the Messenger ﷺ

[41] Sūrat al-Naḥl, Verse 106.

responded: "No, 'Ammār is filled with faith from head to toe; and faith has amalgamated with his flesh and blood."

In this context, the verse above descended. 'Ammār was crying, so the Messenger of God ﷺ dried out his tears from his eyes and said: "If they come back to you, repeat to them what you have said."[42]

2. Al-Zamakhshari said: It was narrated that people from Makkah were afflicted, upon which they abandoned Islam after adopting it. Some were forced to speak words of disbelief while they were faithful believers. Some of them were 'Ammār b. Yāsir and his parents: Yāsir and Sumayyah, Ṣuhayb, Bilāl and Khabbāb.

As for 'Ammār, He verbally gave them what they wanted unwillingly.[43]

---

[42] Ṭabrisī, Shaykh Faḍl b. Ḥasan, *Majma' al-Bayān fī Tafsīr al-Qur'ān*, Vol. 3, p. 388.

[43] al-Zamakhsharī, *al-Kashshāf 'an Ḥaqā'iq at-Tanzīl*, Vol. 2, p. 430.

3. Al-Hafiz Ibn Maja said: Giving means agreeing with the disbelievers on what they demanded as a practice of Taqiyyah. In this case, Taqiyyah is permissible due to His ﷻ saying: ﴾*barring someone who is compelled while his heart is at rest in faith*﴿[44,45]

4. Al-Qortobi said: al-Ḥasan said: Taqiyyah is permissible for Man until the Day of Resurrection. Then, he said: Scholars agreed that whoever is compelled to disbelieve out of fear for his life from murder is not said to have sinned if he disbelieved while his heart is at rest with faith.[46] His wife does not get divorced from him, nor is he sentenced as a disbeliever. This is the opinion of Mālik, the Kūfis, and al-Shāfiʿī.[47]

5. Al-Khāzin said: Taqiyyah does not stand unless it is accompanied by fear of getting

---

[44] Sūrat al-Naḥl, Verse 106.

[45] Muḥammad b. Mājah al-Qazwīnī, *Sunan Ibn Mājah*, Vol. 1, p. 53, the explanation of ḥadīth number 150.

[46] Sūrat al-Naḥl, Verse 106.

[47] al-Qurṭubī, *Tafsīr al-Qurṭubī: al-Jāmiʿ Li Aḥkām al-Qur'ān*, Vol. 4, p. 57.

killed on the one hand and a good intention on the other. God ﷻ said: ﴾*barring someone who is compelled while his heart is at rest in faith*﴿[48] Thus, this Taqiyyah is permissible.[49]

6. al-Khaṭīb ash-Shirbīnī said: ﴾*barring someone who is compelled*﴿[50] which implies verbal pronunciation, and ﴾*while his heart is at rest in faith*﴿[51] thus he is not accountable for anything; since the heart is where faith resides.[52]

7. Ismāʿīl al-Ḥaqqi said: ﴾*barring someone who is compelled*﴿[53] means he was forced to verbalize something out of fear for his life or one of his organs. This is because disbelief is a matter of core belief, whereas compulsion

---

[48] Sūrat al-Naḥl, Verse 106.

[49] al-Baghdādī, Alī b. Muḥammad Khāzin, *Tafsīr al-Khāzin*, Vol. 1, p. 277.

[50] Sūrat al-Naḥl, Verse 106.

[51] Ibid.

[52] *al-Sirāj al-Munīr*, the interpretation of the verse.

[53] Sūrat al-Naḥl, Verse 106.

is related to speech rather than belief. Thus the meaning is clarified as follows: "However, he who is forced to disbelieve in speech" ﴾*while his heart is at rest in faith*﴿[54] isn't considered to have a changed belief. This is proof that the faith that saves a person and is taken into consideration by God believes by heart.[55]

The Second Verse:

God ﷻ said:

﴿لا يَتَّخِذِ الْمُؤمِنونَ الكافِرينَ أَولِياءَ مِن دونِ الْمُؤمِنينَ ۖ وَمَن يَفعَل ذٰلِكَ فَلَيسَ مِنَ اللَّهِ في شَيءٍ إِلّا أَن تَتَّقوا مِنهُم تُقاةً﴾

﴾*lā yattakhidhi l-mu'minūna l-kāfirīna 'awliyā'a min dūni l-mu'minīna wa-man yaf'al dhālika fa-laysa mina llāhi fī shay'in 'illā 'an tattaqū minhum tuqātan*﴿

[54] Ibid.

[55] al-Barūsawī, Ismā'īl Ḥaqqī, *Tafsīr Rūh al-Bayān*, Vol. 5, p. 84.

﴾*The faithful should not take the faithless for allies instead of the faithful, and God will have nothing to do with those who do that, except when you are wary of them, out of caution*﴿[56]

In this regard, the words of the scholars are sufficient and do not require further clarification.

1. Al-Ṭabarī said: ﴾*except when you are wary of them, out of caution*﴿[57] Abū al-'Aliya said that Taqiyyah is by speech, not action. Imām al-Ḥusayn told me: I heard Aba Ma'ath say: Obeid told us: I heard al-Dahhak say in God's ﷻ saying: ﴾*except when you are wary of them, out of caution*﴿[58]: Taqiyyah is by speech. He who is forced to say something which is considered as disobedience to God ﷻ out of fear for himself ﴾*while his heart is at rest in faith*﴿[59]

[56] Sūrat Āl 'Imrān, Verse 28.

[57] Sūrat Āl 'Imrān, Verse 28.

[58] Sūrat Āl 'Imrān, Verse 28.

[59] Sūrat al-Naḥl, Verse 106.

then he is not considered to have sinned; for, Taqiyyah is but a matter of speech.[60]

2. Al-Zamakhsharī said in regards to the interpretation of God's ﷻ saying: ﴾*except when you are wary of them, out of caution*﴿[61]: He allowed them to take the faithless as allies if they feared them. The intended meaning behind this allegiance is that any rising objection or relationship thereof is merely apparent. Meanwhile, the heart rests in enmity, hatred, and anticipation of the removal of this obstacle.

3. Ar-Rāzī said in regards to interpreting God's ﷻ saying: ﴾*except when you are wary of them, out of caution*﴿[62]: the fourth matter: Know that Taqiyyah has many provisions of which we will mention some:

a. Taqiyyah occurs when the person lives with faithless people he fears for his life and wealth. So, he humors them through his

---

[60] al-Ṭabarī, Muḥammad, *Jāmiʿ al-Bayān*, Vol. 3, p. 153.

[61] Sūrat Āl ʿImrān, Verse 28.

[62] Sūrat Āl ʿImrān, Verse 28.

words, that is, by not showing enmity through speech. It is even permissible for him to speak words that instill the delusion of love and allegiance on the condition that he conceals the opposite and – internally – objects to what he says. For, Taqiyyah influences the exterior rather than the condition of the hearts.

b. Taqiyyah is permissible in pursuit of safeguarding one's self. Is it permissible to protect one's wealth? It is possible to have a ruling that says that it is permissible due to His ﷻ saying: "The sanctity of a Muslim's wealth is like that of his blood", and the saying of the Prophet ﷺ: "He who is killed for his wealth is a martyr."

4. Al-Nasfī says: ﴿*except when you are wary of them, out of caution*﴾[63] unless you fear that which must be averted from them. This refers to the case where a disbeliever has power over you whereby you fear him for yourself and wealth, upon which you are

[63] Sūrat Āl 'Imrān, Verse 28.

permitted to show allegiance to him and conceal enmity against him.[64]

5. Al-Ālūsī said: The verse holds proof for the legitimacy of Taqiyyah. They defined it as safeguarding the self, honor, or wealth against the enemy's wickedness. An enemy is of two sorts:

First: He whose enmity is based on the difference in religion, such as the Muslim and the disbeliever.

Two: He whose enmity is based on worldly purposes, such as wealth, amusement, possessions, and dominance.[65]

6. Jamāl al-Dīn al-Qāsimī said: From this verse ﴾*except when you are wary of them, out of caution*﴿[66], the Imāms deduced the legitimacy of Taqiyyah during moments of fear. Murtaḍā al-Yamānī mentioned, in his

---

[64] *Tafsīr al-Nasfī* in the footnotes of *Tafsīr al-Khāzin*, Vol. 1, p. 277.

[65] *Tafsīr Rūḥ al-Ma'ānī*, Vol. 3, p. 121.

[66] Sūrat Āl 'Imrān, Verse 28.

book (*Ithār al-Ḥaqq 'ala al-Khalq*), that there was a unanimous opinion about the legitimacy of Taqiyyah during such circumstances.[67]

7. Al-Māraghi interpreted the verse ﴿*except when you are wary of them, out of caution*﴾[68] by saying that the believers' abandonment of their allegiance to the disbelievers is an absolute necessity in all situations except for the case of fear from that which they dread from them. Thus, the legal principle is "Averting damage takes precedence over attaining benefits."

Whereby it is permissible for them to give allegiance to disbelievers to avert harm, it is even more so in pursuit of benefitting the Muslims. Accordingly, it is not problematic for a Muslim country to ally with a non-Muslim country to acquire a pursued advantage for the former by preventing harm or acquiring a benefit. However, it is not permissible for the former to

---

[67] al-Qāsimī, *Tafsīr al-Qāsimī: Maḥāsin al-Ta'wīl*, Vol. 4, p. 82.

[68] Sūrat Āl 'Imrān, Verse 28.

ally with the latter in anything that harms Muslims. This alliance is not restricted to circumstances of weakness; it is always permissible.

The scholars concluded, from this verse, the legitimacy of Taqiyyah, that is, for a person to speak or act in violation of righteousness in pursuit of averting harm from the enemy onto himself, his honor, or wealth.

For, he who utters a word of disbelief - under force - in pursuit of shielding himself from death, while his heart rests with faith, is not considered a disbeliever. He is excused for his actions, as was the case with ʿAmmār b. Yāsir, whom Quraysh forced to disbelieve upon which he agreed unwillingly – while his heart was restful in faith. The following verse referred to him: ﴾Whoever renounces faith in God after [affirming] his faith —barring someone who is compelled while his heart is at rest in faith﴿[69,70]

[69] Sūrat al-Naḥl, Verse 106.

[70] al-Māraghi, Aḥmad Muṣṭafa, *Tafsīr al-Māraghi*, Vol. 3, p. 136.

These specific and comprehensive words do not leave room for doubt in the legitimacy of Taqiyyah according to its definition, as mentioned above. It is almost impossible to find an interpreter or a scholar who questioned its concept or purpose without hesitation in confirming its legitimacy. Moreover – Dear Reader – you will not find a mindful person who would not practice it during difficult circumstances as long as it does not give rise to much corruption – as will be elaborated further as we study its limitations.

He who objects to its permissibility or questions its legitimacy perceives it as the trendy form of Taqiyyah, which is common amongst secretive organizations and destructive sects such as the Esoteric (*Batiniyya*) and their likes. Nonetheless, all Muslims are innocent of this form of Taqiyyah which is destructive of every noble virtue.

The Third Verse:

God ﷻ said:

﴿وَقالَ رَجُلٌ مُؤمِنٌ مِن آلِ فِرعَونَ يَكتُمُ إِيمانَهُ أَتَقتُلونَ رَجُلًا أَن يَقولَ رَبِّيَ اللَّهُ وَقَد جاءَكُم بِالبَيِّناتِ مِن رَبِّكُم ۖ وَإِن يَكُ كاذِبًا فَعَلَيهِ كَذِبُهُ ۖ وَإِن يَكُ صادِقًا يُصِبكُم بَعضُ الَّذي يَعِدُكُم ۖ إِنَّ اللَّهَ لا يَهدي مَن هُوَ مُسرِفٌ كَذّابٌ﴾

﴿wa-qāla rajulun mu'minun min 'āli fir'awna yaktumu 'īmānahū 'a-taqtulūna rajulan 'an yaqūla rabbiya llāhu wa-qad jā'akum bi-l-bayyināti min rabbikum wa-'in yaku kādhiban fa-'alayhi kadhibuhū wa-'in yaku ṣādiqan yuṣibkum ba'ḍu lladhī ya'idukum 'inna llāha lā yahdī man huwa musrifun kadhdhāb[un]*﴾*

﴿Said a man of faith from Pharaoh's clan, who concealed his faith, 'Will you kill a man for saying, "My Lord is God," while he has already brought you manifest proofs from your Lord? Should he be lying, his falsehood will be to his own detriment;

but if he is truthful, there shall visit you some of what he promises you. Indeed God does not guide someone who is a profligate, a liar﴾[71]

---

[71] Sūrat Ghāfir, Verse 28.

The consequences of his actions were the following:

﴿فَوَقاهُ اللَّهُ سَيِّئاتِ ما مَكَروا ۖ وَحاقَ بِآلِ فِرعَونَ سوءُ العَذابِ﴾

﴿fa-waqāhu llāhu sayyi'āti mā makarū wa-ḥāqa bi-'āli fir'awna sū'u l-'adhābi﴾

﴿Then God saved him from their evil schemes, while a terrible punishment besieged Pharaoh's clan﴾[72]

This was only because through practicing Taqiyyah, he managed to save the Prophet of God from death:

﴿قالَ يا موسىٰ إِنَّ المَلَأَ يَأتَمِرونَ بِكَ لِيَقتُلوكَ فَاخرُج إِنّي لَكَ مِنَ النّاصِحينَ﴾

﴿qāla yā-mūsā 'inna l-mala'a ya'tamirūna bika li-yaqtulūka fa-khruj 'innī laka mina n-nāṣiḥīna﴾

﴿He said, 'Moses! The elite are indeed conspiring to kill you. So leave. I am indeed your well-wisher.'﴾[73]

---

[72] Sūrat Ghāfir, Verse 45.

[73] Sūrat al-Qaṣaṣ, Verse 20.

These verses indicate the permissibility of practicing Taqiyyah to save a believer from the evil of his disbelieving enemy.

Taqiyyah in the Prophetic Sunnah

Narrations referred to the fact that the permissibility and prohibition of an act become inapplicable during cases of compulsion – such as Taqiyyah. The most evident proof is the ḥadīth of "lifting accountability during compulsory situations," narrated by the two groups.

1. Shaykh Ṣadūq mentioned a narration – of a correct (ṣaḥīḥ) chain – in his book 'al-Khiṣāl' on behalf of Imām al-Ḥusayn ؑ where he said: The Messenger of God ﷺ said, "(The pen) is lifted off my nation in nine situations: error, forgetfulness, what they were forced to do, what they cannot endure, what they do not know, what they were compelled to do out of necessity, envy, pessimism and contemplating on the internal devious whispers about creation as long as it does not transfer into words."[74]

This ḥadīth plays a role in the study of exemption (barā'ah) and occupation (ishtighāl) in the principles of jurisprudence (Uṣūl al-

---

[74] Ṣadūq, Shaykh Muḥammad b. 'Alī, al-Khiṣāl, p. 417.

Fiqh), and we elaborated on it in our studies thereof.[75]

In any case, the ḥadīth is clear that necessity makes the prohibited permissible.

2. Al-Kulaynī narrated, with a correct chain of narrations, on behalf of Zurāra, on behalf of Imām Jaʿfar al-Ṣādiq ﷺ that he said, "Taqiyyah (is permissible) in every necessity; and the person involved in it knows best when this necessity befalls him."[76]

3. Al-Kulaynī narrated on behalf of Muḥammad b. Muslim and Zurāra said: We heard Imām Jaʿfar al-Ṣādiq ﷺ say, "Taqiyyah exists in every necessity that befalls man; for God made it permissible for him."[77]

4. It is narrated that Imām Jaʿfar al-Ṣādiq ﷺ said, "Every act performed by a believer, in the cases that require Taqiyyah, is

[75] Irshād al-Uqūl, Vol. 1, p. 347-364.

[76] al-Ḥurr al-ʿĀmilī, Shaykh Muḥammad b. al-Ḥasan, *Wasāʾil al-Shīʿa*, Vol. 11, ch. 25, ḥadīth number 1.

[77] Ibid, ḥadīth number 2.

permissible as long as it does not cause any corruption in religion."[78]

5. It is also narrated that Imām Jaʿfar al-Ṣādiq ﷺ said, "No perjury takes place, and no atonement is due to the person who swears while practicing Taqiyyah to prevent harm from inflicting him."[79]

6. It is narrated that Imām Jaʿfar al-Ṣādiq ﷺ said, "Taqiyyah is wider than that which lies in between the earth and sky."[80]

These are some of several narrations that are mentioned in this regard.

One can add, as evidence, the verses which allowed for certain acts during times of necessity; for God ﷻ said:

---

[78] Kulaynī, Shaykh Muḥammad b. Yaʿqūb, *Al-Kāfi*, Vol. 2, p. 168.

[79] Ṣadūq, Shaykh Muḥammad b. ʿAlī, *al-Khiṣāl*, p. 607.

[80] Majlisī, ʿAllamah Muḥammad Bāqir, *Biḥār al-Anwār*, Vol. 75, p. 412.

﴿فَمَنِ اضطُرَّ غَيرَ باغٍ وَلا عادٍ فَلا إِثمَ عَلَيهِ ۚ
إِنَّ اللَّهَ غَفورٌ رَحيمٌ﴾

﴾fa-mani ḍṭurra ghayra bāghin wa-lā ʿādin fa-lā ʾithma ʿalayhi ʾinna llāha ghafūrun raḥīmun﴿

﴾But should someone be compelled, without being rebellious or aggressive, there shall be no sin upon him. Indeed God is Forgiving, Merciful﴿*[81]

This verse – though it comes in the context of hunger – tackles the issue of necessity, be it an internal factor such as eating carrion or an external one that forces people to act in a way which – if not abided by – will cause them and their valuables harm.

---

[81] Sūrat al-Baqarah, Verse 173.

* According to some exegetical traditions, *bāghī* refers to one who rebels against a just ruler (according to another interpretation, to a hunter), and *ʿādī* refers to a thief or highwayman (see Ṭabarī, Rāzī, *al-Tafsīr al-Burhān*). Cf. 6:145; 16:115.

Taqiyyah in the Words of Scholars

1. Ibn ʿAbbās said: Taqiyyah is practiced by the tongue while the heart is restful in faith, and the person does not reach out to kill.[82]

2. Al-Ḥasan al-Basrī said: Taqiyyah is permissible for a believer until the Day of Resurrection except for killing a soul.[83]

3. Al-Rāzī said: that Taqiyyah is permissible in pursuit of safeguarding one's wealth, and it is permissible to safeguard one's self.[84]

4. Al-Suyūṭī said: Eating carrion with one's fingers, dipping one's food in liquor, and speaking words of disbelief – though prohibited wholly without carrying any trace of permissibility save rarely – are permissible to fulfill what is needed.[85]

---

[82] al-ʿAsqalānī, Ibn Ḥajar, *Fath al-Bāri*, Vol. 12, p. 279.

[83] *Tafsīr al-Naysabūrī* in the footnotes of Muḥammad al-Ṭabarī, *Tārīkh al-Ṭabarī*, Vol. 3, p. 178.

[84] *Tafsīr al-Kabīr*, Vol. 8, p. 13.

[85] *al-Ashbāh wal-Naẓā'ir*, p. 76.

5. Al-Shāṭibī condemned the Khawārij for denying Taqiyyah in speech and action. He considered it part of their violations of general religious principles – original or practical.[86]

6. Shaykh Muḥammad ibn Ḥasan Ṭūsī said: Taqiyyah, according to us, is mandatory in the event of fear for one's life. A narration mentions that he has allowed for the permissibility of disclosing righteousness therein.[87]

7. ʿAllamah Ṭabātabāʾī said: The Noble Qurʾān and the Sunnah agree on its permissibility in general. Reason upholds this stance; religion has no purpose, and its Legislator has no concern besides the emergence and nourishment of religion. It may be that practicing Taqiyyah and humoring the enemies of religion and those who violate righteousness preserve religion's interests

---

[86] al-Shāṭibī, Ibrāhīm b. Mūsā, *al-Muwāfaqāt fī Usūl al-Sharīʿa*, Vol. 4, p. 180.

[87] Ṭūsī, Shaykh Muḥammad b. Ḥasan, *al-Tibyān fī Tafsīr al-Qurʾān*, Vol. 2, p. 435.

and the sustainability of righteousness more than forsaking and denying it out of arrogance and abuse.[88]

The Scope of Taqiyyah in Personal Affairs

The Shīʿas were known for practicing Taqiyyah in their speech and actions; thus, it has become a basis for a delusion that stuck in the minds of some superficial and fallacious people who said: Since Taqiyyah is one of the Shīʿa principles, then it is not right to rely on what they say, write and publish. For, it is quite possible that their books are mere advertisements while their reality is otherwise. This is what we keep hearing from them. It is repeated frequently by the Pakistani writer Iḥsān Ilāhī Ẓahīr in his sick books in which he attacked Shīʿas.

However, we want to draw the reader's attention to Taqiyyah's scope, which is restricted to partial and personal matters in the event of fear for one's life and valuables. Accordingly, if the evidence implies that showing one's beliefs or implementing the Ahl

[88] Ṭabāṭabāʾī, ʿAllamah Sayyid Muḥammad Ḥusayn, *al-Mīzān fī Tafsīr al-Qurʾān*, Vol. 3, p. 153.

al-Bayt عليهم السلام school will cause the believer harm, it becomes a place for Taqiyyah. Both reason and the Sharīʿa demand the duty of being wary in pursuit of safeguarding one's self and valuables from danger. The general matters that fall outside the realm of fear are not befitting for Taqiyyah. The books that the Shīʿas publish are included in the latter category; for, when the person is writing, he does not do so out of fear so that it may be permissible for him to write in contrast to what he believes as he does not need to write in the first place. He can remain quiet and refrain from writing anything.

These people's claims that the Shīʿa books are advertisements rather than facts arise from their lack of knowledge of the reality of Taqiyyah for Shīʿas.

In conclusion, Shīʿas used to practice Taqiyyah when they didn't have a state that protected them, not any power or shield preventing danger from befalling them. As for the current times, there is not any justification or excuse for resorting to Taqiyyah except for specific and partial matters.

Shīʿas, as we have mentioned, resorted to Taqiyyah only under the pressure of necessity. It is a right that I do not think anyone – who thinks with his mind rather than his feelings – would deny. Nonetheless, it is a given across Shīʿa history that the rulings that allowed for Taqiyyah were plenty, yet, on the practical level, Shīʿas were the most sacrificial people. Any researcher can simply review the stances taken by Shīʿa men with Muʿāwīya b. Abī Sufyān, other Umayyad rulers, and ʿAbbāsid rulers such as Ḥijr b. ʿUday, Maitham al-Tammār, Rashīd al-Ḥijrī, Kumayl b. Zīyād and hundreds of others, in addition to the stances taken by the followers of Imām ʿAlī ﷺ throughout history and their consecutive revolutions which were mentioned in some chapters.

The Categories of Taqiyyah

Based on the division of rulings, Taqiyyah is divided into five categories, of which it is important to mention three.

1. Obligatory Taqiyyah: It is that by which one averts fear for a respectable self or honor or intolerable harm that would otherwise befall him or other believers.

2. Recommended Taqiyyah: It is that by which one averts what is preferably averted of slight damage, which is usually tolerable, whether it is related to himself or others.

3. Prohibited Taqiyyah: it results in even greater corruption, such as the destruction of religion, concealing the truth from the upcoming generations, and the enemy's dominance over Muslims' affairs, sanctities, and mosques. That is why many of the great Shīʿas rejected Taqiyyah in certain situations and sacrificed themselves for the sake of religion. For, Taqiyyah has its place – but so does the prohibited part of it as well.

Taqiyyah, at its core, is the concealment of what one dreads to show until the danger is gone, for it is the best route to be saved from brutality.

However, that does not mean that a Shīʿa is a coward who lacks determination and is scared, hesitant, and humiliated. Not at all. For, Taqiyyah has its limitations which it must not trespass. As it is obligatory in some instances, it is also prohibited in others. Taqiyyah in front of an oppressive ruler like Yazīd b. Muʿāwīya b. Abī Sufyān, for example, is prohibited; for it would result in humiliation, disgrace, abandonment of values, and decline. The permissibility and impermissibility of Taqiyyah do not depend on strength and weakness; the interests of Islam and Muslims instead determine them.

Āyatullāh Sayyid Khumaynī ﷾ spoke about Taqiyyah, and we will present his words as they are so the reader can reflect that Taqiyyah has specific provisions and might be prohibited from upholding higher interests. He said:

Practicing Taqiyyah is prohibited in specific prohibitions and obligations which represent – according to the legislator – a high position, such as the destruction of the Kaʿbah and the honorable landscapes, and countering Islam, the Noble Qur'ān, and its exegesis by that which corrupts the sect and resembles atheism and other significant prohibitions. In these cases, the proofs of Taqiyyah, necessity, and compulsion do not apply.

In the respectable ḥadīth by Mas'ada b. Ṣadaqa, one can find proof for the above: "Every act committed by a believer in practicing Taqiyyah is permissible, as long as it does not result in the corruption of religion."[89]

One of the cases that fall under this category is the case of a person who has a high stance and position in people's eye, whereby committing specific prohibitions or abandoning certain obligations out of Taqiyyah may weaken the sect and violate its sanctities – such as being forced to drink liquor or commit fornication. In these cases, holding on to Taqiyyah on the premise of the proof of lifting accountability[90]. The proof of Taqiyyah is problematic – nay, forbidden.

---

[89] al-Ḥurr al-ʿĀmilī, Shaykh Muḥammad b. al-Ḥasan, *Wasā'il al-Shī'a*, Vol. 10, ch. 25, ḥadīth number 8.

[90] al-Ḥurr al-ʿĀmilī, Shaykh Muḥammad b. al-Ḥasan, *Wasā'il al-Shī'a*, Vol. 10, ch. 25, ḥadīth number 1.

Most importantly, the impermissibility of Taqiyyah reaches its peak when one of the original principles of Islam or the sect - or a necessity thereof - is at risk of demise, destruction, and alteration, such as – for example – the case where the oppressive perverts would want to change the provisions of inheritance, divorce, prayer, pilgrimage, and other original provisions, in addition to the origins of religion or the sect. Taqiyyah, in these cases, is impermissible. Its legislation aimed at preserving the sect and the original principles and bringing together the scattered Muslims to establish religion and its original principles. Thus, if things were to reach the destruction of this religion, then Taqiyyah would be rendered impermissible. This – though clear – is manifested in the document above.[91]

In light of the above, we conclude the following:

1. Taqiyyah is a Qur'ānic principle that the Prophetic Sunnah upholds. When the Islamic message was being disseminated,

---

[91] A letter on Taqiyyah printed out amongst the ten letters: Vol. 14, the chapter on areas excluded from the proofs.

Taqiyyah was practiced by the afflicted companions in pursuit of safeguarding themselves. The Messenger ﷺ did not object to their action; on the contrary, he supported them through Qur'ānic verses – as in the case of ʿAmmār b. Yāsir, whereby the Prophet ﷺ asked him to repeat what he said if they came back at him.

2. Taqiyyah does not correspond to establishing secret societies for sabotage and destruction. This does not have anything to do with Taqiyyah.

3. Interpreters agreed - when interpreting the verses related to Taqiyyah – to adopt the same conclusion as the Shīʿas regarding the permissibility of Taqiyyah.

4. Taqiyyah is divided into five categories based on the rulings' division. Whereby it is obligatory in some instances, we find it forbidden in others.

5. The scope of Taqiyyah does not exceed personal matters. It only applies where fear

exists, whereas when fear and pressure cease
to exist, then Taqiyyah no longer applies.

In conclusion of our study, we say:

We assume that Taqiyyah is a crime committed
by a person to preserve his blood, honor, and
wealth. The crime dwells in the reason which
imposes Taqiyyah on the Shī'a Muslim and leads
him to say or act against his beliefs. He who
condemns the persecuted Muslim for practicing
Taqiyyah must allow him to be free in his life
and leave him alone. The most he can do –
within reasonable standards – is to ask him for
proof of his beliefs and source of action. If he
turns out to be following valid proof, he follows
him. If not, he excuses himself in his *Ijtihad* and
scientific and intellectual efforts.

We invite Muslims to contemplate the motives
that pushed the Shī'as towards Taqiyyah and
work on giving space to their brothers in
religion, for every Muslim scholar has his
opinion, perception, efforts, and potential.

Shī'as follow the footsteps of the Imāms of Ahl
al-Bayt 🕮 in regard to beliefs and the Sharī'a

and adopt their opinions; for they are the ones from whom God ﷻ repelled impurities and whom He ﷻ purified with a thorough purification. They are one of the two weighty things the Messenger ﷺ ordered to hold on to regarding beliefs and Sharīʿa. Their beliefs are not concealed from anyone; it is proof to all.

We ask God ﷻ to protect the blood of Muslims and their honor from any violation, unify their lines, harmonize their hearts, bring them together, and make them one line in the face of the enemy. He has the power to do that and is eligible to respond.

Suspicions Around Taqiyyah

You were introduced to the reality of Taqiyyah, in terms of language, terminology, and history, as you have learned its proofs in the Noble Qur'ān and the Sunnah. It was also shown to you that it was a common practice by Muslims to resort to Taqiyyah during difficult times. Nonetheless, some suspicions remain around Taqiyyah, which we will raise for discussion.

First Suspicion: Taqiyyah is a Form of Hypocrisy

Whereby Taqiyyah means to show the opposite of what the heart conceals or acts contrary to one's beliefs, it is then considered a form of hypocrisy. Hypocrisy means to act outwardly contrary to one's beliefs.

The response to this is quite clear: The concept of Taqiyyah in the Noble Qur'ān and the Sunnah demands the display of disbelief and concealment of faith or falsehood and concealment of righteousness. Whereby this is its meaning, the difference between Taqiyyah and hypocrisy is between faith and disbelief. For, hypocrisy is its exact opposite; it is the display of faith and concealment of disbelief, and the display of righteousness and concealment of falsehood. In light of this difference, thus, Taqiyyah must not be considered a form of hypocrisy.

In other words: Hypocrisy, in religion, is the concealment of disbelief at heart, and the display of faith by the tongue. This is so far from Taqiyyah! Instead, it is its exact opposite ﴿*barring someone who is compelled while his heart is at rest in faith*﴾[92] For, it is the display of disbelief and the cover-up and concealment of faith at heart. As for the Shīʿas' Taqiyyah, it entails the concealment of one's belief in the Imāmate and Guardianship of Ahl al-Bayt عليهم السلام, which means to hide the identity of being a Shīʿa while pretending to agree with others on their beliefs about Imāmate. At the same time, they join the Muslims in their two testimonies and their belief in the Resurrection. They also practice their worship rites, act upon the subsidiary parts of religion, believe in them wholeheartedly, and live this belief system with their hearts and souls.

---

[92] Sūrat al-Naḥl, Verse 106.

Yes, those who defined hypocrisy as any discord that occurs between the appearance and the core, and, accordingly, considered Taqiyyah – which was mentioned in the Noble Qur'ān and Sunnah – as one of its branches had interpreted as a more expansive concept than that mentioned in the Noble Qur'ān which defined hypocrites as those who pretend to be believers and conceal their disbelief:

﴿إِذَا جَاءَكَ الْمُنَافِقُونَ قَالُوا نَشْهَدُ إِنَّكَ لَرَسُولُ اللَّهِ ۗ وَاللَّهُ يَعْلَمُ إِنَّكَ لَرَسُولُهُ وَاللَّهُ يَشْهَدُ إِنَّ الْمُنَافِقِينَ لَكَاذِبُونَ﴾

﴿'idhā jā'aka l-munāfiqūna qālū nashhadu 'innaka la-rasūlu llāhi wa-llāhu ya'lamu 'innaka la-rasūluhū wa-llāhu yashhadu 'inna l-munāfiqīna la-kādhibūna[a]﴾

﴿When the hypocrites come to you

they say, 'We bear witness

that you are indeed the apostle of God.'

God knows that you are indeed His Apostle,

and God bears witness that

the hypocrites are indeed liars.﴾[93]

Suppose this is the definition of a hypocrite. How can it be compared to those who practice Taqiyyah in front of disbelievers and transgressors, whereby they conceal their faith or adherence to Ahl al-Bayt ﷺ and show their agreement (with the transgressor) in pursuit of safeguarding themselves, their valuables, honor and wealth from violation?

We will realize the validity of those mentioned earlier when reflecting on the fact that it was legislated in Islam. Had it been a form of hypocrisy, it would have been a heinous thing that would never be allowed by a wise being:

﴿قُل إِنَّ اللَّهَ لا يَأمُرُ بِالفَحشاءِ ۖ أَتَقولونَ عَلَى اللَّهِ ما لا تَعلَمونَ﴾

﴿*qul ʾinna llāha lā yaʾmuru bi-l-faḥshāʾi ʾa-taqūlūna ʿalā llāhi mā lā taʿlamūn*[a]﴾

[93] Sūrat al-Munāfiqūn, Verse 1.

❨Say, 'Indeed God does not enjoin indecencies. Do you attribute to God what you do not know?'❩[94]

The Second Suspicion: Why was Taqiyyah Considered among the Original Principles of Religion?

It was narrated on behalf of the Imāms of Ahl al-Bayt 🕮 that they said, Taqiyyah is my religion and the religion of my fathers, and he who does not practice Taqiyyah has no religion.[95]

From the look of it, believing in Taqiyyah and practicing it is one of the original principles of religion, whereby he who does not practice it steps out of religion and has no share of faith within.

The comment to be noted in this regard is that Taqiyyah is one of the jurisprudential topics subjected to the five rulings - like all other topics thereof. Thus, it is sometimes obligatory and

---

[94] Sūrat al-Aʿrāf, Verse 28.

[95] al-Ḥurr al-ʿĀmilī, Shaykh Muḥammad b. al-Ḥasan, *Wasāʾil al-Shīʿa*, Vol. 10, ch. 24, ḥadīth 3, p. 22.

other times prohibited at certain times. Accordingly, how can it be an original principle of religion when the Shīʿa scholars mentioned it under the chapter of Enjoining Good and Forbidding Evil (*al-Amr bil-Maʿrūf wal-Nahy ʿanil-Munkar*)?

Concerning the narrations that considered it to be of the principles of religion, their reference was metaphoric; and it aimed at emphasizing the importance of believing in it and practicing it in life to protect one's self and valuables. Since some of the Shīʿas used to speak overtly about their beliefs and rites – which led to their arrest, torture, and bloodshed, the Imām – in order to avert such consequences – said that "Taqiyyah is my religion and the religion of my fathers," all in pursuit of encouraging them to follow their footsteps. As for the statement "He who does not practice Taqiyyah has no religion," it emphasized the practice of Taqiyyah, similar to his saying: The prayer of one who neighbors a mosque is not accepted except inside the mosque.

In other words, the reference to the term "religion" does not mean the original general principles such as Monotheism (*Tawḥīd*), Prophethood, and the Hereafter, which upon believing in them, one becomes a Muslim, and upon denying them one – or one of them or that which is associated with one of them – steps out of Islam. What was meant by using the term "religion" was that through which the Imām worships and acts upon the religion of God. His saying, "Taqiyyah is my religion and the religion of my fathers," implies that it is of our affairs – the Ahl al-Bayt 🕮 – therefore, follows our footsteps. As for the person who assumes that Taqiyyah violates his dignity, he is ignorant and said to have stepped outside the religious way of the Imāms 🕮.

The Third Suspicion: Taqiyyah Leads to the Annihilation of Religion

Suppose a group of people practices Taqiyyah, for a long time, in the original principles of religion and its subsidiaries. In that case, the upcoming generation might view their fathers' practice as an intrinsic part of religion and its reality. Thereupon, Taqiyyah will lead to the annihilation of religion and its fading.

The comment to be noted in this regard is that Circumstances vary and are not of one sort. For, pressure may intensify upon which the righteous do not find a means to express his opinion, beliefs, and laws. However, circumstances may change to more appropriate conditions which allow for the practice of one's rites freely. The Shīʿas have lived in these different circumstances at different times in history. By doing so, they protected their original and subsidiary principles and culture. God ﷻ has been the ultimate Supporter who preserved this religion and its laws.

In other words: Taqiyyah controls the exterior and not the core. The minorities whose liberties have been confiscated practice Taqiyyah outwardly. In their private gatherings, they attend to their obligations as needed and raise their children upon the teachings inherited from their fathers, who have taken their knowledge from their Imāms عليهم السلام.

If we assume that adopting Taqiyyah for an extended period will result in the annihilation of religion, then Taqiyyah – in this case – would be forbidden and abstained from. It has been mentioned earlier that Taqiyyah has five rulings, whereby the Taqiyyah that leads to the annihilation of religion is forbidden.

The Fourth Suspicion: Taqiyyah Leads to the Suspension of Enjoining Good (*al-Amr bil-Maʿrūf*)

Taqiyyah is an idea that transforms a Muslim into a human being who adapts to reality with all its oppression, corruption, and perversion. It goes back to being content with the surrounding oppression, corruption, and perversion.

The comment to be noted in this regard is the following: Enjoining good and forbidding evil are obligations conditional on one's ability to fulfill them. These obligations are carried out at two levels. One level is the role of the individual, which is enjoining good through efforts toiled by the heart and tongue. Another level is the role of the community – on top of which is the state which has the power and strength to do so. He who practices Taqiyyah enjoins good and forbids evil based on his capacity. Thus, where there is no capacity or accountability, God ﷻ

does not burden a soul with more than it can bear.

Despite that, those practicing Taqiyyah await the opportunities to attack and change the corrupt reality. Had the circumstances supported this change, they would have forsaken Taqiyyah and proclaimed the truth out loud through speech and action.

The Fifth Suspicion: Practicing Taqiyyah in Front of a Muslim is Heresy

Some may assume that Taqiyyah is a Shīʿa invention and that it does not have any base in the Noble Qurʾān and the Sunnah; for the verses mentioned in regards to Taqiyyah are related to Muslims being wary of disbelievers. As for a Muslim practicing Taqiyyah in front of another Muslim, no evidence supports it in the Noble Qurʾān and the Sunnah.

The comment to be noted in this regard is the following: Even though the verses addressed a Muslim's wariness of a disbeliever, the reference was not restricted to the verse. When afflicted with disbelievers, legislating Taqiyyah aims to safeguard oneself and valuables from evil. Therefore, if a Muslim is afflicted with his Muslim brother who disagrees with him on some subsidiary principles, and the powerful party does not hesitate to harm the other party by torturing him, robbing him of his wealth, or killing him, then common sense demands, in these sensitive circumstances, that one protects himself and his valuables by concealing his beliefs and practicing Taqiyyah. If someone needs to be held accountable, then it should be the one whose evil is being averted rather than the one who is practicing Taqiyyah. We believe that if freedom was widespread amongst all the Islamic groups, and all these groups tolerated others' opinions, then they would perceive these opinions as fruits of their Ijtihād. Thereupon, none of the Muslims would need to practice Taqiyyah; and harmony would prevail instead of conflict.

Some scholars understood that and spoke of it. Below are the words of some of these scholars:

1. Al-Shāfiʿī said: Taqiyyah amongst Muslims is permissible, as it is amongst disbelievers, in pursuit of self-protection.[96]

2. Al-Rāzī said in his interpretation of God's ﷻ saying: ﴾*except when you are wary of them, out of caution*﴿[97]: The exterior of this verse indicates that Taqiyyah takes place in front of dominant disbelievers. However, the Shāfiʿī sect considers that when the condition amongst Muslims resembles that between Muslims and disbelievers, Taqiyyah becomes applicable as a means of self-defense. He also said: Taqiyyah is permissible to safeguard one's self; is it permissible to safeguard one's wealth? He likely considers it permissible due to the Prophet's ﷺ saying: "The sanctity of a Muslim's wealth is similar to the sanctity of his blood", and his ﷺ saying: "He who is

---

[96] *Tafsīr al-Naysabūrī* in the footnotes of Muḥammad al-Ṭabarī, *Tārīkh al-Ṭabarī*, Vol. 3, p. 178.

[97] Sūrat Āl ʿImrān, Verse 28.

murdered while protecting his wealth is a martyr."[98]

3. Jamāl al-Dīn al-Qāsimī narrates on behalf of Murtaḍā al-Yamāni his words in his book '*Ithār al-Ḥaqq 'ala al-Khalq*': Two things made righteousness more vague and invisible: One of them is the Gnostics' fear – though they are few – of wicked scholars, oppressive rulers, and devious people, accompanied by the permissibility of Taqiyyah, during these situations, in the Noble Qur'ān and according to the unanimous opinion of Muslims. Fear remains an obstacle to disclosing righteousness, and the righteous person is an enemy to most people. It is narrated that Abū Hurayrah said – in regards to the first Islamic period: I learned, from the Messenger of God ﷺ, two vessels (of knowledge): I transmitted one of them to

[98] ar-Rāzī, Fakhr ad-Dīn, *Mafātīḥ al-Ghayb*, Vol. 8, p. 13, on the interpretation of this verse.

the people; and had I transmitted the other, I would have had my throat slit.[99]

4. Al-Māraghi said in his interpretation of the verse: ﴿*barring someone who is compelled while his heart is at rest in faith*﴾[100]: Humoring disbelievers, oppressors, and debauchees falls under Taqiyyah, in addition to being lenient in speech while talking to them, smiling at them and offering them money as means to protect one's self and honor from them. This is not considered a form of forbidden allegiance to them; instead, it is legal. Al-Ṭabarānī stated, then, the Prophet's ﷺ saying: "Whatever a believer uses as a means to protect his honor is considered as alms."[101]

The Shīʿas are wary of disbelievers in specific circumstances for the same reason Sunnīs dread them. However, the Shīʿa – for evident reasons

---

[99] al-Qāsimī, *Tafsīr al-Qāsimī: Maḥāsin al-Ta'wīl*, Vol. 4, p. 82.

[100] Sūrat al-Naḥl, Verse 106.

[101] al-Māraghi, Aḥmad Muṣṭafa, *Tafsīr al-Māraghi*, Vol. 3, p. 136.

– resorts to practicing Taqiyyah in front of his Muslim brother, not due to any shortcoming in the former but rather in his brother, who pushed him in that direction. He knew he would be tortured and killed if he declared his beliefs which he aligns with the original principles of the Islamic Sharīʿa and its theologies. Yes, the Shīʿa – up until most recently – used to avoid saying: God ﷻ does not have a side, or He will not be seen on the Day of Resurrection, or the political and knowledgeable reference after the beloved Prophet ﷺ is Ahl al-Bayt ﵃, or the ruling of temporary marriage (*mutʿah*) has not been nullified. If a Shīʿa declares any of these facts – that were deducted from the Noble Qurʾān and the Sunnah – he will expose himself and his valuables to demise and dangers. You have been presented with the frank words of al-Razi, Jamal al-Dīn al-Qāsimī, and al-Māraghi on the permissibility of this kind of Taqiyyah. Restricting Taqiyyah to that practiced in front of a disbeliever is a form of a rigid interpretation of the verse at its surface level, closing doors to deeper understanding, rejection of the core reason for which Taqiyyah was legislated, and eradicating the rule of reason which dictates that one must preserve the most important when it conflicts with the less important.

It has been mentioned that many elite narrators resorted to Taqiyyah during difficult times, which almost destroyed their lives and property. The best example in this regard is the one mentioned by al-Ṭabarī in his book '*Tarīkh al-Ṭabarī*', where al-Ma'mūn attempts to push the judges and narrators in his time towards admitting – unwillingly – to the idea that the Noble Qur'ān was created, and whereby they knew that denying this proposition would lead to the murder of everyone without any mercy. When those narrators saw the sword's sharpness, they pretended to agree with al-Ma'mūn's proposition and concealed their beliefs in their hearts. Later, when they were blamed for agreeing with al-Ma'mūn, they justified their action by referring to 'Ammār b. Yāsir who was forced to display polytheism while his heart rested in faith. This story is famous and clear about the permissibility of resorting to Taqiyyah. The Shī'ass were condemned as if they invented the concept themselves without basing it on any fixed and well-known Islamic rules and original principles.

The Constructive Effects of Taqiyyah

If tyranny prevailed in a human society where liberties were confiscated, rights violated, and voices of the free silenced. The deprived minorities will not have any means left besides resorting to Taqiyyah and coexisting with reality. Although some people perceive this issue as undesirable, Amīr al-Mu'minīn ﷺ – as will be mentioned – describes it as a permit that God ﷻ has gifted to believers. Practicing Taqiyyah resulted in constructive effects that can be summed up as follows:

Preserving One's Self and Valuables

Practicing Taqiyyah and humoring the tyrannical oppressor safeguards the minorities from the brutality, suppression, murder, and confiscation of money – contrary to abandoning this practice which exposes them to murder and demise. That is why it is referred to as a shield or a weapon. Imām Ja'far al-Ṣādiq ﷺ said, "Taqiyyah is a believer's shield, and he who does not practice Taqiyyah is faithless."[102]

---

[102] al-Ḥurr al-'Āmilī, Shaykh Muḥammad b. al-Ḥasan, *Wasā'il al-Shī'a*, Vol. 11, ch. 24, ḥadīths 6 and 7.

He ﷷ also said, "My father used to say: Nothing brings me tranquility more than Taqiyyah; for, Taqiyyah is a believer's weapon."[103]

Shaykh al-Mufīd narrated the following: ʿAlī b. Yaqṭīn (the Shīʿa minister of Hārūn al-Rashīd) wrote to Imām Mūsā al-Kāẓim ﷷ and asked him about ablution, to which the Imām ﷷ responded, "I understood what you mentioned in regards to the differences in ablution. What I order you to do now in this matter is to gargle three times, inhale three times, wash your face three times, soak your beard in vinegar, wash your hands from fingers to elbows three times, wipe your head entirely, wipe the external and internal parts of your ears, wash your feet until the ankles three times and do not breach any of this to adopt another.

When ʿAlī b. Yaqṭīn received this letter, he was surprised at Imām Mūsā al-Kāẓim ﷷ response which the Shīʿas unanimously rejected. Then he said: My Master is more knowledgeable, and I will abide by his command. He performed ablution by those standards and, accordingly,

---

103 Ibid.

Rashīd tested him without making him suspicious. When he watched how he performed his ablution, al-Rashīd called him and said: He is a liar who claimed you to be a Shīʿa. Thereupon, ʿAlī b. Yaqtīn was well-regarded by al-Rashīd. He then received a letter from Imām Mūsā al-Kāẓim ﷺ saying: "Start now, O' ʿAlī b. Yaqtīn, perform ablution in the way God ﷻ ordered you. Wash your face once as an obligation and once as a recommended act, then wash your arms from the elbows, wipe the top-front part of your head, and wipe your feet with the leftover due from your ablution. For what we feared for you has faded. Peace."[104]

Preserving the Unity of the Nation

There is no doubt that the nation's unity is the source of this nation's power and flourishing. It is the tight rope of God ﷻ which must be held, whereby He ﷻ said in His Noble Qur'ān:

﴿وَاعْتَصِمُوا بِحَبْلِ اللَّهِ جَمِيعًا وَلَا تَفَرَّقُوا﴾

[104] al-Ḥurr al-ʿĀmilī, Shaykh Muḥammad b. al-Ḥasan, *Wasāʾil al-Shīʿa*, Vol. 1, ch. 32, ḥadīth 3.

﴿*wa-ʿtaṣimū bi-ḥabli llāhi jamīʿan wa-lā tafarraqū*﴾

﴿*Hold fast, all together, to God's cord, and do not be divided [into sects]*﴾[105]

God ﷻ considered segregation, fragmentation, and scattering as a form of agony that uproots a nation and exhausts its powers. God ﷻ said:

﴿قُل هُوَ القادِرُ عَلىٰ أَن يَبعَثَ عَلَيكُم عَذابًا مِن فَوقِكُم أَو مِن تَحتِ أَرجُلِكُم أَو يَلبِسَكُم شِيَعًا وَيُذيقَ بَعضَكُم بَأسَ بَعضٍ﴾

﴿*qul huwa l-qādiru ʿalā ʾan yabʿatha ʿalaykum ʿadhāban min fawqikum ʾaw min taḥti ʾarjulikum ʾaw yalbisakum shiyaʿan wa-yudhīqa baʿḍakum baʾsa baʿḍin*﴾

﴿*Say, 'He is able to send upon you a punishment from above you or from under your feet,*

or confound you as [hostile] factions, and make you taste one another's violence.'﴾[106]

[105] Sūrat Āl ʿImrān, Verse 106.

[106] Sūrat al-Anʿām, Verse 65.

These are some of many other verses that encourage unity and warn against division and scattering.

Legislating Taqiyyah supports unity and saves the nation from getting scattered. That is why the Imām describes it as "a permit which God ﷻ gifted the believers out of mercy for them."

This means that one can practice Taqiyyah sparingly; if appropriate opportunities were available for him to express his opinion and way of life, practicing Taqiyyah becomes forbidden because it results in the effacement of religion and the concealment of truth.

Maintaining the Faculties and Protecting them from Exhaustion

Through practicing Taqiyyah, the deprived groups protect their faculties and potential from being thoroughly exhausted. Therefore, they raise people who are conscious of their goals. When freedom befalls them, they are ready to openly express their ideas and opinions without fear or intimidation, in addition to demanding their rights. These are some of the effects of Taqiyyah which safeguarded vulnerable people from complete exhaustion of their faculties.

Since these constructive effects are a clear manifestation of mercy, to which the Amīr al-Mu'minīn referred, we will present his words below:

Al-Sharīf al-Raḍī narrated in his letter '*al-Muhkam wal-Mutashabih*', on behalf of *Tafsīr al-Nu'mānī*, on behalf of Imām 'Alī ﷺ, that he said, "God gifted the believer with the permit to practice Taqiyyah externally – to fast when he fasts, breaks his fast when he breaks his, prays in compliance with his prayers, acts upon his actions and shows him this behavior elaborately. Internally, however, he must adopt the religion of God contrary to what he exhibits externally to those he fears as the transgressors who took control over the nation. God gifted this permit to the believers, out of His bounty and mercy, so they can use it while practicing Taqiyyah externally."[107]

---

[107] al-Ḥurr al-'Āmilī, Shaykh Muḥammad b. al-Ḥasan, *Wasā'il al-Shī'a*, Vol. 1, ch. 25, ḥadīth 1.

www.ingramcontent.com/pod-product-compliance
Lightning Source LLC
Chambersburg PA
CBHW031422120626
46545CB00006B/2240
* 9 7 8 1 9 5 6 2 7 6 3 4 3 *